Carnival Glass

THE BEST OF THE BEST

IDENTIFICATION GUIDE TO RARE AND UNUSUAL PIECES

Bill Edwards & Mike Carwile

COLLECTOR BOOKS
A Division of Schroeder Publishing Co., Inc.

On the Front Cover
Acorn Burrs punch set, aqua opalescent, 12" tall

On the Back Cover
Millersburg Multi-Fruits and Flowers
punch bowl, tulip shaped, cobalt blue

Cover design by Beth Summers
Book design by Kelly Dowdy

COLLECTOR BOOKS
P.O. Box 3009
Paducah, Kentucky 42002-3009

www.collectorbooks.com

Acknowledgments

To thank all those whose photos appear in this book is a problem since many of these pictures have been in our files for as much as three decades, some even going back to that first book, *Millersburg, Queen of Carnival Glass*. A good example that we are using for the first time is the wonderful Acorn Burrs aqua opal punch set, or the rare Dugan Cherry chop plate; Don Moore sent me both of these photos many years ago, writing on the back what he'd paid for them at the time. I have always remembered Don by his many kindnesses over the years as only friends can be remembered.

So to be fair, we are listing only those who have recently sent in photos or e-mailed them to Mike just for this book. To all the others, we offer our thanks and appreciation for all their help over the years.

Current thanks go to Don and Becky Hamlet, Randy and Jackie Poucher, Kathy and Quindy Robertson, Steve Maag, Harold and Delores Wagner, Alan and Lorraine Pickup, John and Rayann Calai, Tito Norris, Mike Young, Jerry Kudlac, Mr. and Mrs. Chuck Hollenbach, Alan Sedgwick, Gary Lickver, Casy Rich, Tom and Sharon Mordini, David Davis Antiques, Inc., Jim Wroda, and Dr. Jack Adams.

Introduction

When our publisher suggested we do a book of this scope, covering the "best of the best," top collector favorites in carnival glass, we were very excited. Here we could gather the rare, the unusual, the big bucks glass so very desirable to collectors and so very attractive to newcomers collecting this wonderful glass. Such a book would be educational and show the general public items that often do not come out of private collections for decades and almost never go to public auction. In addition, those of us not fortunate enough to have the wherewithal to put together such glass in our collections could at least marvel at the items shown and set our goals and hone our interests in some day owning some of these items.

So it is with great pleasure that we took on this task and hope this first major book of its kind will please both old and new collectors. We welcome comments and suggestions, as well as information about rare and desirable items we haven't been able to show in this book, but may be able to display in the future.

Prices of items in this book will usually range from the low $1,000s to more than 100 times that much and for that reason, we do not price this glass. In addition, while we acknowledge the help of collectors in our acknowledgments we do not attribute any particular piece or pieces of glass to a collector, believing that most who own these rare and expensive items would prefer remaining unnamed.

Finally, we've decided to use only glass made by American companies in this book. We realize there are rare and desirable carnival glass items from other countries but our space had to be governed by practicality and for that reason, there is no foreign glass (to the best of our knowledge) shown here. Perhaps that would be a topic for another book at another time, but even with these self-imposed limits, we wish we could show more pieces than time and space permits. We hope readers will be able to look through this book and quickly spot trends that make some carnival pieces desirable.

Absentee Dragon

Evidently a prototype of the Dragon and Berry pattern, this very rare 9" plate has the berries but not the dragons. It is one of two reported and created quite a stir when it was first found. The exterior pattern is the typical Fenton's Bearded Berry and the coloring and iridescence are excellent.

Acorn Burrs Aqua Opal Punch Set

Acorn Burrs is one of Northwood's best patterns. This rare punch set in aqua opalescent glass rates just behind the Grape and Cable set in the same treatment. Northwood originally called this pattern "Chestnut" and began production in 1910 in berry sets, table sets, water sets, and punch sets. The rare aqua opalescent pieces came along in 1912 or 1913 and only three punch sets (as well as some odd parts) are reported in this color. To own even one cup in aqua opalescent glass is a real treat and the complete set shown has to be a collector's dream come true.

Acorn Burrs Blue Punch Set

While cups in blue have been known for some time, the matching bowl and base was first sold to a carnival glass collector in 2001, and it is a rare and desirable beauty. As in the case of the aqua opalescent pieces in this shape and pattern, the blue set joined the very elite of iridized punch sets. We understand Northwood called this cobalt color "royal blue." It wasn't one of their most-produced colors; but it certainly is one of their purest, being a bright true blue. At any rate, the blue punch set is a real treasure.

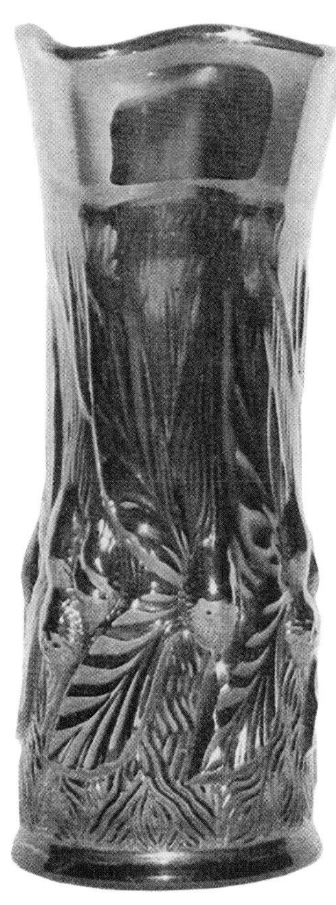

Acorn Burrs Vase

This rare vase whimsey that was pulled or swung from the tumbler shape, can be found in marigold as well as the amethyst shown. This example is 7½" tall. The marigold example is similar and to date only the two have been reported, but since the tumbler has been found in green, the possibility of a green vase whimsy does exist.

Acorn Compote (Millersburg)

Millersburg added their own interior pattern to this compote whose mould came originally from the Crystal Glass Company when that factory closed in 1908. The Acorn compote can be found in ruffled or deep straight-sided versions and the colors reported are marigold, amethyst, green, and vaseline. Marigold is actually the rarest with only one known, but the other colors are also very rare with only two or three of each reported.

Acorn Plate

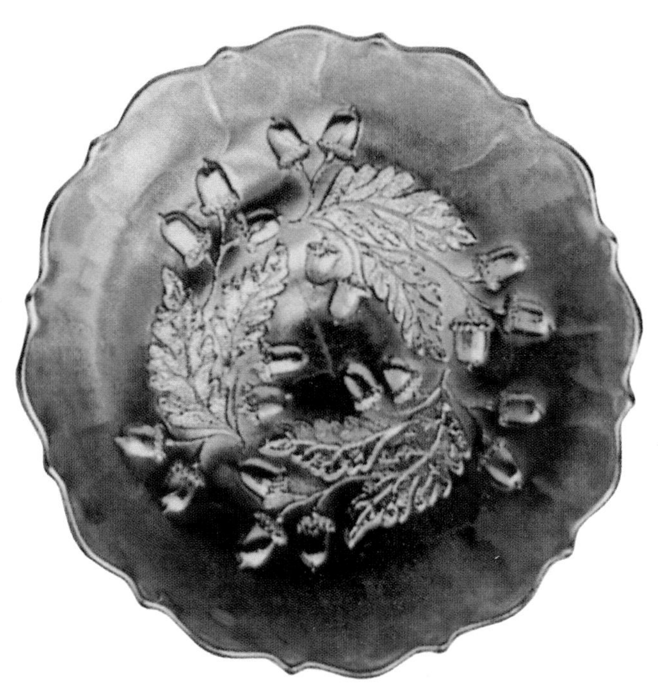

In bowls this is a prolific pattern from the Fenton Art Glass Company, but the very rare plates are a different matter. To date, three cobalt blue (two are damaged), two marigold, and one amethyst are known. Measuring about 9" in diameter, these plates show the design to its best advantage and to own one is a collector's dream.

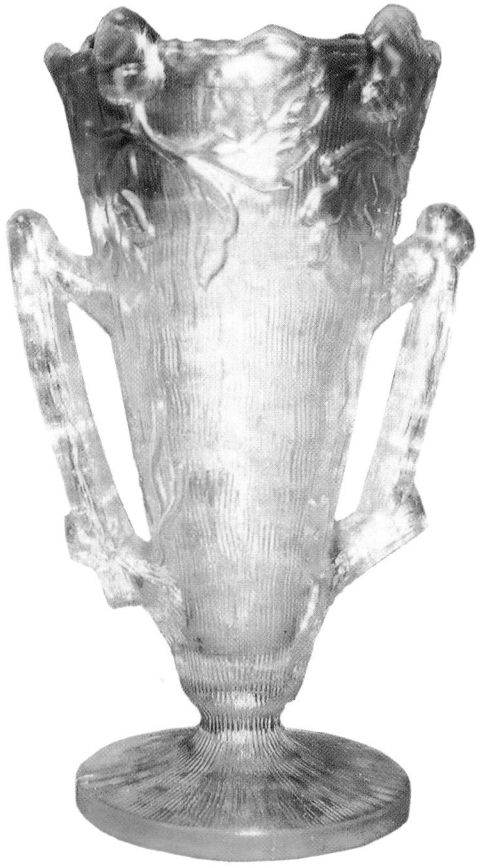

Acorn Vase

This very rare vase was once believed to have been a product of the U.S. Glass Company, but current evidence of shards found at the site of the old Millersburg plant now indicate this may well be a rare vase from the Millersburg Glass Company. To date, only one vase in each of the marigold, amethyst, green, and vaseline colors are known. The vase is relatively small at about 5½" tall. It has two twig handles with a bark-like surface over much of the bowl, stem, and base and there are acorns, leaves, and vines that wind around and over the top. Shown is the beautiful vaseline example but any of the colors is truly a treasure.

Age Herald

This Fenton bowl and plate pattern is found in amethyst only. The bowls can be ruffled or ice cream shape. It is also called Birmingham Age Herald because it was designed as a giveaway for the Alabama newspaper. This well-designed pattern is a real collectors' favorite and is very scarce, especially the plates.

Apple Tree Vase

This rare vase whimsey, shaped from the pitcher whose handle was omitted (note the blank rectangle above and the circle below where the handle would have gone), is known in marigold, cobalt blue, or uniridized crystal. The top rim can be flared or ruffled as in the example shown and estimates indicate that fewer than three or four whimsies are known in each color.

Banded Grape and Cable Orange Bowl

Sometimes called a fruit bowl, this seldom-found large, deep, footed bowl comes with the banding just below the top (rarer) and without it. It is normally found only in marigold or cobalt blue, but here we have a very rare iridized opaque slag glass that ranges in color from rusty red to a yellow-lime color. It is the only example reported so far and is a very desirable item. The owner calls this treatment mustard-custard.

Bellflower (Fuchsia)

This quite rare handled compote from Fenton was first named Bellflower by one owner and then Fuchsia by the next. Colors are marigold or cobalt blue and both are very limited, bringing high prices whenever sold, even if damaged.

Bernheimer Bowl

This advertising bowl configured from the same mould as Millersburg's Many Stars pattern is found only in blue carnival glass, is about 10" across, and has the Trefoil Finecut exterior. The lettering reads "Bernheimer Brothers" and the large star of Many Stars is replaced by a smaller star. The Bernheimer bowl is a real favorite and brings a hefty price when sold.

Big Fish Banana Boat

This well designed piece is one of collectors' favorite Millersburg bowl patterns. It is usually found in round or ruffled bowls (a squared bowl exists) but here is one of the rare banana bowl (or boat) shapes. It is a fantastic piece, found in amethyst, vaseline, and green (one example of each has been reported).

Big Fish Rose Bowl

This seldom-seen, very beautiful rose bowl whimsy from Millersburg is found on a single marigold, a single amethyst (shown) and the beautiful vaseline bowl (shown). Like the other whimsey shapes in this pattern (tri-cornered bowl, square bowl, banana bowl), the rose bowl is a collectors' favorite and is much sought after.

Big Fish Tri-Cornered Bowl

Found in marigold, amethyst, or green, this tri-cornered bowl with a candy ribbon edging is real collectors' favorite in any pattern but in the Big Fish it becomes a rare thing of beauty. The finish is Millersburg's usual radium, and only a few examples are known in each color.

Big Thistle

Many collectors consider this the very best designed punch bowl and it is easy to see why. Only two examples of this Millersburg masterpiece are known and neither has cups. A third bowl and base has long been reported but not confirmed. Both sets are amethyst with a fine radium iridescence. One bowl is flared and has a bit of damage and the other is straight sided. The exterior is Millersburg's Flute or Wide Panel design.

Bird Galaxy

Only two of these strange vases are reported at this time — one in green carnival glass and the watery white carnival shown. The vase is 10¼" tall, with a pinched neck. It has an array of birds that are said to be a peacock, heron, pheasant, and a flamingo, but on close examination, the birds seem to be strange imaginative creatures.

Blackberry Bark Vase

Like the Acorn vase, this rare pattern (three known) was first thought to be a U.S. Glass product but it now seems to be a Millersburg pattern. All known examples are amethyst and have a pedestal base. The body is covered with a bark-like surface, with fruit and leaves winding above and along the lip, rising where berries and leaves extend. Both rare and desirable, this vase grabs your attention from the start and is a collectors' dream. Please note that one vase is more flared than the other.

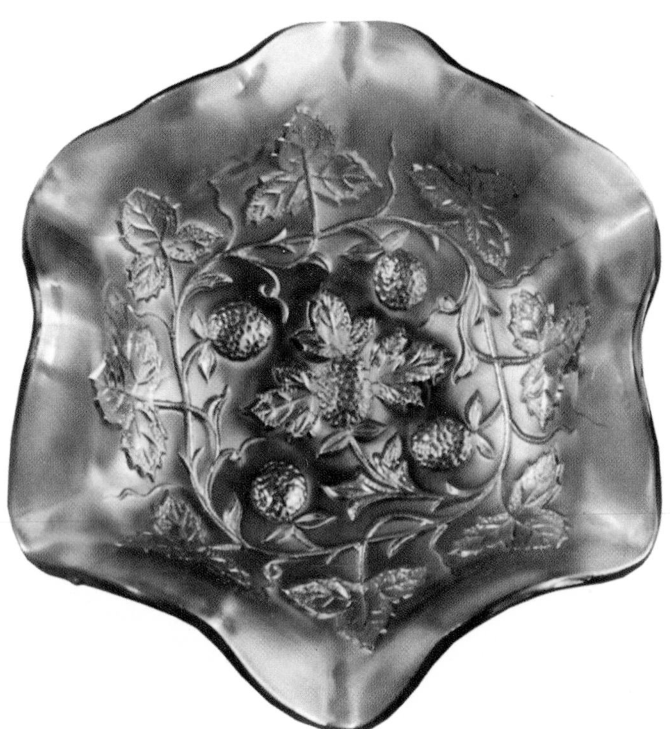

Blackberry Wreath (blue)

This Blackberry Wreath pattern is from Millersburg and is easy to find in marigold, amethyst, or green, but to locate one in vaseline or the rare blue shown is a real task. Blue bowls are known in the 7" ruffled bowl shown, a 10" ruffled bowl, and a 10" ice cream shaped bowl. Only two or three of the small bowls are found in this color and each has a radium finish.

Blackberry Wreath Decorated Bowl

Millersburg had some of the best experimental or decorated pieces of carnival glass and this is no exception. It is a marigold bowl with ruffled edges. The leaves are gilded with gold and the berries are gilded with copper or bronze. The bowl is the small sauce size and needless to say is a fine rarity.

Blackberry Wreath Plate

Found in three sizes, the Blackberry Wreath plates from Millersburg are very rare and much coveted. The 6" size (shown) is found in marigold (seven known), amethyst (five reported); the single 8" plate is in green, and the chop plate (10½") is reported in amethyst (two) and marigold (one).

Blackberry Wreath Small Spittoon

Shaped from a small marigold sauce bowl in Millersburg's Blackberry Wreath pattern, this very tiny spittoon whimsey is a rare, rare find, only recently coming to light. It has a very strong marigold color with a radium finish and a flute or wide panel exterior.

Brazier's Candies

Made by the Fenton Art Glass Company as one of their many advertising pieces, the Brazier's Candies pattern is found in bowls, plates, and a hand-grip plate. All are found in amethyst. While not nearly as rare or costly as many items in this book, these advertising pieces are desirable and always cause spirited bidding when sold.

Broeker's Flour

Thus far this Northwood advertising piece has been seen only in a plate shape and in amethyst carnival glass. It is perfectly plain except for the lettering which reads: "We use Broecker's Flour," and is a bit hard to find.

Brooklyn Bridge (unlettered)

This commemorative piece was made late in carnival glass (after1928) by the Diamond Glass Company in marigold, pink with marigold iridescence, and gilded marigold. Most pieces are lettered below the Zeppelin but some rare examples (three are now reported) do not have this lettering like the example shown. Bowls can be six, eight, or ten ruffled and most have a strong iridescence.

Butterfly (with threaded exterior)

Just why Northwood used two different exterior patterns on this compote is a mystery but the Threaded exterior brings the interest and the cost up greatly. Colors for this variation are marigold, amethyst, green, cobalt blue, and the rarest of the colors, the ice blue shown.

Butterfly and Berry Spittoon

There are actually two spittoon whimsies shaped from the footed bowl in this Fenton pattern. The second is taller than the example shown and stands on its feet while the one has the feet splayed outward and sits on its collar base. Both are amethyst and very desirable.

Butterfly and Corn Vase

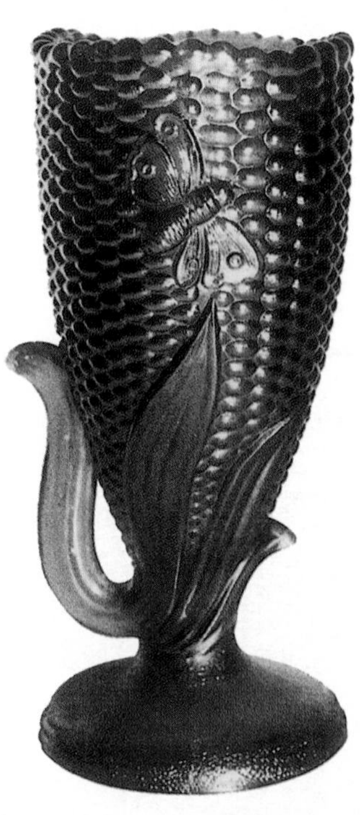

The recent discovery of shards from the Millersburg plant site indicates this wonderful pattern was from that company, with one example each of marigold, vaseline, green, and amethyst known (the green vase is now broken). These vases are about 6" tall and have a base diameter of 2¾". The pedestal bases are stippled, and above them corn shucks wind around the vase with one solid husk looped out and away from the ear. Above the top husk, a moth-like insect hovers. The corn kernels are very realistic and end at the top in uneven rows. Anyone lucky enough to own one of these rare beauties is fortunate indeed.

Butterfly and Tulip

Certainly not as rare as most of the items in this book, the Butterfly and Tulip footed bowl relies on its massive size and impressive design to grab the interest of collectors. It can be found on deep round bowls as well as the more desirable shallower squared bowls. Colors are marigold or amethyst with the latter more important. The exterior has the Inverted Fan and Feather pattern (inherited from Northwood) and the maker is Dugan.

Butterfly Tumbler

Also known as Big Butterfly by some collectors, this very rare tumbler was a product of U.S. Glass and was part of a water set in crystal. Just why only the tumblers were later made in iridized glass is a mystery. At any rate, here we show one of the four or five known green examples and there is also a single marigold tumbler in a Texas collection. The design is a good one with four large butterflies on a stippled background. Above and below are indented circles and below the top row are fans with beaded edges.

Campbell & Beesley Spring Opening

This rare and very collectible advertising plate from the Millersburg Glass Company is found on hand-grip plates in amethyst. The plate says "Campbell & Beesley-Spring Opening-1911." The firm it advertised is said to be a ladies apparel store in Nashville, Tennessee.

Caroline Bowl (amethyst)

Found with the usual Smooth Rays interior (shown), this rare bowl with the Caroline exterior is from 1910 and was made by Dugan. Previously reported in only in marigold, peach opalescent, lavender opalescent, or decorated carnival, this example is in a true amethyst and is the first reported in this color.

Central Shoe Store

The plate shown was also made in a handgrip plate and bowls by Fenton. The letter says "Compliments of the Central Shoe Store — Collinsville and St. Louis Ave's East-St. Louis, III."

Chatalaine

This very rare water set is a work of art. It is known only in purple carnival (water sets were made in 1909 in uniridized crystal also) and was first seen in iridized glass in 1912. Marigold pieces have long been rumored but none are known. Smoke would certainly be a possibility if other colors were indeed made.

Checkerboard Water Set

This pattern was called Old Quilt by Westmoreland and in carnival glass it can be found only on a goblet, punch cup, and the water set pieces shown. Tumblers, the goblet, and punch cups are found in amethyst and marigold but the pitcher is known in only amethyst. (Water sets have been reproduced using the old moulds by L.G. Wright, so be very careful.) It is estimated that three or four old pitchers are known. The example shown is more lavender than amethyst.

Cherry Chain Chop Plate

This majestic 11" chop plate is shown with one of Fenton's better known bowl patterns. It can also found on a 6½" plate. It is found in both white and marigold but the latter seems to be the most desirable. It certainly wouldn't surprise anyone to see a blue one show up (one Fenton author lists both blue and green). It has been reproduced.

Cherry Chop Plate

Previously unreported, this Dugan Cherry chop plate (10½" diameter) is a rarity that boggles the mind. It was shaped from the large bowl mould and has a fantastic satiny iridescence that is filled with gold highlights. The exterior is the Jeweled Heart pattern as usually found on these pieces. This photo has been in our files since Don Moore sent it to me many years ago and apparently hasn't seen the light of day until now.

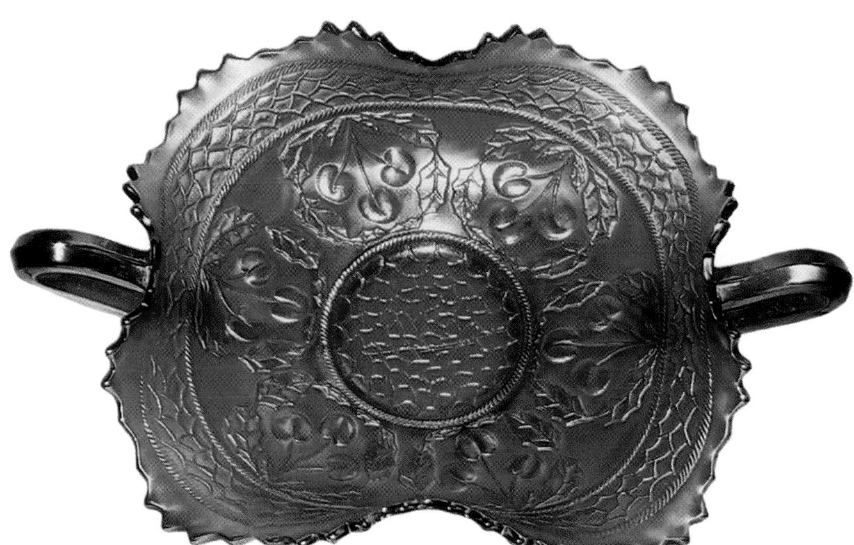

Cherry Circles Bonbon (red)

This large bonbon was made by Fenton in 1920 as their #1426 pattern. It is found in round, square, or banana boat shapes, in marigold, amethyst, green, blue, aqua, white, horehound, ice blue, or the scarce red shown.

Cherry Compotes

While the standard compotes from Millersburg are rare, these two whimsied shapes are ultra-rare with only one in each shape reported. Both are amethyst and roughly 7½" tall. One has the ends pulled out making it into a banana boat shape and the other is squared on four sides with only a slight flaring. This pattern is also known as Hanging Cherries by some collectors but Millersburg Cherry was the original name.

Cherry/Hobnail Bowl

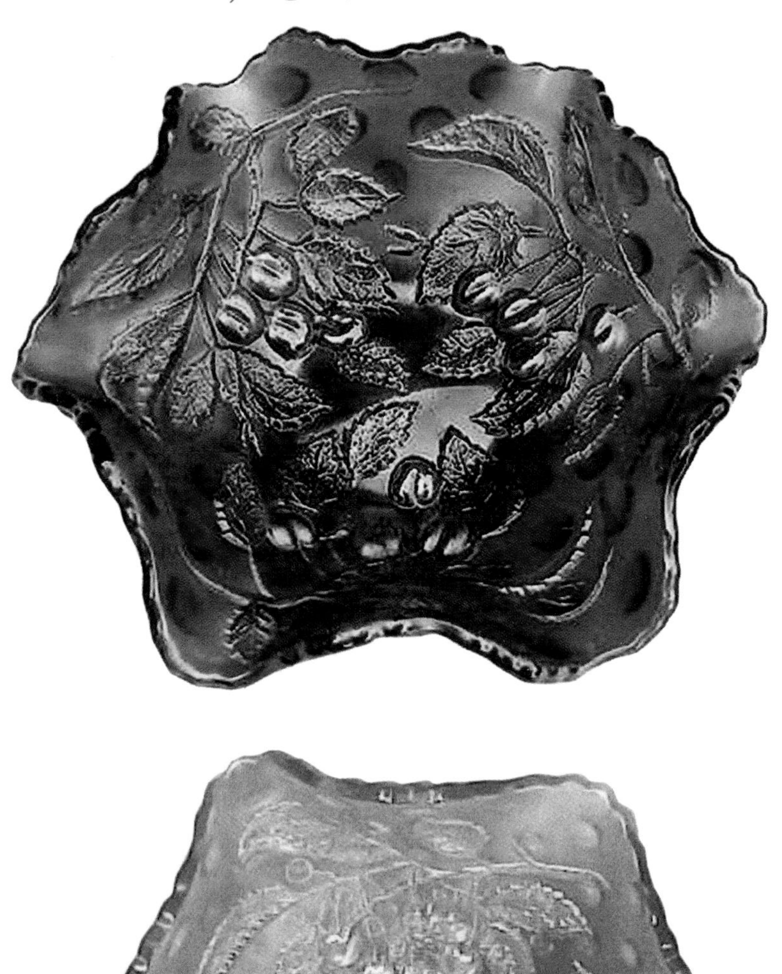

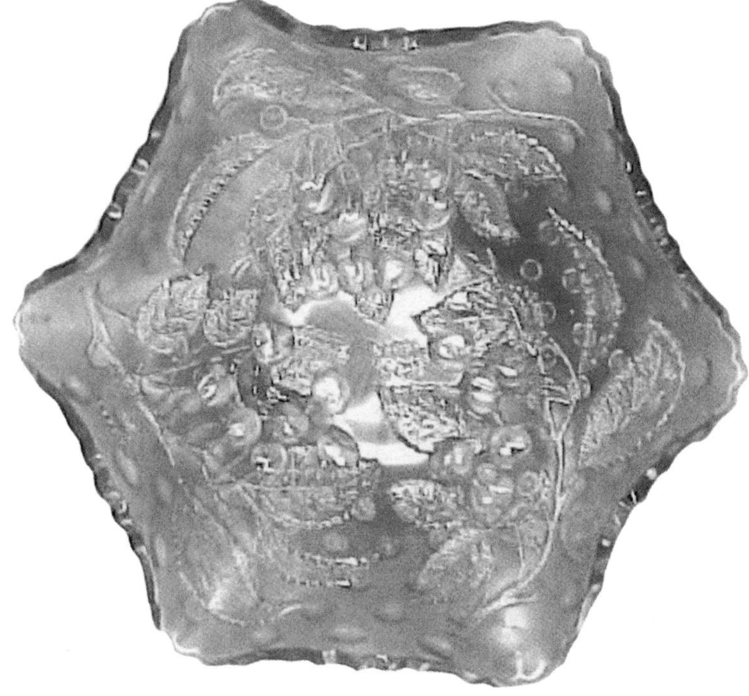

These 9½" bowls, on one of Millersburg's seldom discussed patterns, are very rare and desirable in any color. They are found in amethyst (ten or twelve), marigold (five), blue (two or three), and green (one). In addition, there is a small sauce known in blue. The exterior of these bowls is the same mould used with the Vintage/Hobnail pattern with only the interiors changed. Cherry is rarer than the Vintage.

Christmas Compote

This large short-stemmed compote is really quite rare. It is shown on one of the Dugan Glass Company's best loved patterns, which is similar in design to their Holly and Berry pattern. It can be found in amethyst or marigold and either color is very desirable. And while the rediscovered moulds were used to make limited runs of these compotes in non-old colors, the original hasn't suffered.

Cleveland Memorial

This souvenir ashtray was issued to celebrate Cleveland's centennial birthday by the Millersburg Glass Company. Scenes depict James Garfield's tomb, his statue, the Soldiers and Sailors monument, the Superior Street viaduct, and the Chamber of Commerce building. These very rare cigar ashtrays are found in both amethyst and marigold (slightly rarer), and very seldom for sale.

Cone and Tie Tumbler

Long believed by most collectors to be an Imperial pattern, this very rare tumbler has no matching carnival glass pitcher and isn't known in any other color than the purple shown. This rare item is seldom for sale and always brings a high price when sold.

Cooleemee, NC Plate

Tooled from Fenton's well-known Heart and Vine pattern, this 9" plate then served double duty as an advertising piece. It is a rare and much sought item. The lettering reads "Souvenir of Cooleemee, NC. – J.N. Ledford Company." The Ledford Company was a textile mill in North Carolina. The only color reported in this plate is marigold.

Coral

The seldom discussed or sold Coral pattern was made by Fenton as a companion pattern to Little Fishes and Peter Rabbit (they all have the same border treatment). Bowls are found in marigold, green, blue, and vaseline, while plates are reported only in marigold. Bowls still sell for a few hundred dollars but the plate is the rare and desirable item here.

Corn Vase Variant (Northwood)

This third variation of Northwood's Corn vase pattern resembles the Pulled Husk vase but is from a different mould and has the husks pulled out and curled into handle-like projections (it somewhat resembles Dugan's Fancy Husk vase shown elsewhere). Only this single example in amethyst has been reported in seventeen years and it is a real rarity.

Country Kitchen Covered Sugar (vaseline)

Here is a very rare vaseline covered sugar that was part of the Millersburg table set, usually found in marigold or amethyst (all pieces in any color are rare). Besides this piece there are two vaseline spooners reported and that's it. Millersburg's vaseline was as good as anyone's in the business and it is a shame they didn't make more of it in the brief time they were in business.

Country Kitchen Spittoon

Only this single example of this whimsey shape in the Country Kitchen pattern has ever been reported. It is pulled from a spooner shape and is a fiery amethyst with electric iridescence. It first showed up about three decades ago and has seldom been sold and anyone can see why.

Country Kitchen Spooners

Besides the rare vaseline spooners (two are known), this beautiful Millersburg pattern is found in marigold, amethyst, and green, and it is a real privelege to show all three here. All are rare and very desirable. The green is outstanding with its blue iridescence.

Country Kitchen Square Bowl

A favorite with Millersburg collectors, this pattern is usually found as the exterior pattern on Fleur-de-lis bowls, but it is also a primary pattern on berry sets, a table set, and whimsey vases (an example is shown elsewhere). Here is a bowl whimsey shaped from the large berry bowl that measures 10¼" across. It has been pulled into a squared shape and is very rare and desirable.

Country Kitchen Vase

The vase shown, pulled from the spooner shape of Millersburg's Country Kitchen table set, is one of three reported (the other two are taller and pulled even more). All three are a strong marigold color. An amethyst swung vase has also been reported by we haven't seen it.

Courthouse (Millersburg)

While usually found in a bowl called the *lettered* version that says "Millersburg Souvenir" above the building and "Courthouse-Millersburg, Ohio" below, some rare examples do not have the lettering and are called *unlettered* bowls. Shapes can be ruffled, ice cream, or the rarer three-in-one edge. Shown are both lettered and unlettered examples with the three-in one edge shape as well as a lettered ice cream shape. Courthouse bowls are found only in amethyst that can be as light a color as lavender.

Daisy Wreath Vase

A product of the Westmoreland Glass Company, this rare vase whimsey, pulled from a large bowl, is the only one reported at this time. It is marigold, has very good iridescence, and would certainly be a valued addition to any collection of fine glass.

Dance of the Veils

This pattern was called Dancing Ladies by the Fenton Glass Company and was made in many glass treatments. The few known iridized examples are all marigold, and each is a collector's dream. The iridized vases are 8½" tall and can be found ruffled or round. The vase has a very Art Nouveau look with dancing figures and flowing veils.

Davidson's Society Chocolates

This nicely done item is another advertising piece from Northwood that can be found in a hand-grip plate or a double-handgrip plate (sometimes called a card tray). Besides the amethyst shown, pieces can be found in lavender.

Deep Grape

This is one of Millersburg's finest compotes. It can be found round or cone-shaped (amethyst, marigold, green, or blue), squared (marigold, amethyst, or blue), with a twelve-ruffled top with a candy ribbon edge (marigold or amethyst), or in a rose bowl shape (green). The strong pattern is all exterior with grape clusters, leaves, and tendrils like the Millersburg Vintage bowls.

Diamond and Rib Jardiniere

Here is how the large Diamond and Rib vases look before they are swung or pulled into the vase shape. These so-called jardinieres are quite rare and very well liked by collectors. This jardiniere was Fenton's #504 pattern and is known in marigold, amethyst, green, and blue. The base diameter is 5¼" and some examples are flared.

Diamond and Rib Spittoon Whimsey

This rare and desirable spittoon whimsey, from Fenton's well-known vase pattern, was made by pulling the middle in like a corset. At this time two examples are known and both are green, but surely other pieces in this shape may be out there in other colors. This whimsey is made from the smaller base size of this pattern which is known in 3", 3½", and 5½".

Diamond Point Vase (original label)

While this Northwood vase pattern is fairly easy to find in both opalescent glass and the standard colors in carnival glass, there are a handful of items that set collectors wild. The vase shown is one of them. It appears to be a standard vase in amethyst with great color but on the bottom is the original Northwood label! It is the only one reported and is both rare and desirable. Other colors in this vase that stir collectors are rare aqua opalescent and sapphire blue.

Diamond Points Basket

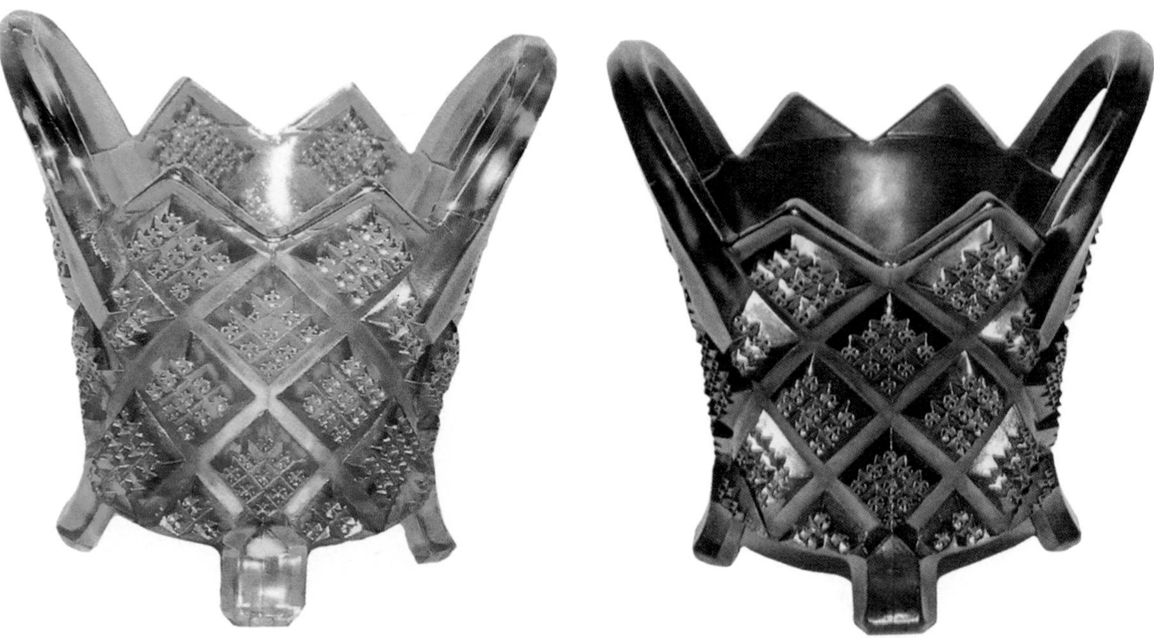

While most collectors believe this basket is from Northwood, there is no concrete evidence of who made it. We do know that it was made in crystal in many, many footed shapes but the four-footed basket with two handles is the only known iridized shape. Colors are marigold, amethyst, and cobalt blue (white has been reported but not confirmed). The Diamond Points basket is rare in any color and creates a buzz when sold.

Diamonds Punch Bowl

Over the years bits and pieces of these sets trickled out until presently one green, one marigold, and one amethyst set (bowl and base only since no cups are known to exist), are now known. Some collectors believe this punch set was a very late entry before the Millersburg plant closed so production didn't really get started. At any rate, these pieces are rare and beautiful and a Millersburg collector's dream. It is a shame more do not exist.

Diamonds Spittoon

Shaped from a Diamonds tumbler from the Millersburg Company, this rare, one-of-a-kind spittoon whimsey created quite a stir and sold for a hefty price in 1994 when it first came to light. It has a fine radium finish on a deep pumpkin marigold. Millersburg made their share of whimsies and all of them seem to be first rate.

Dolphins Compote

Millersburg seemed to have a way with unusual patterns and this rare Dolphins compote typifies that. Colors are mostly green or amethyst on the few known but one rare blue example came to light about 1980 and it is an absolute standout. The Dolphins compote has a Rosalind interior and has a flat plate base that is joined to the compote on a center stem. There are three dolphins that look like they support the bowl.

Double Star Spittoon (Cambridge)

Cambridge was not known for their whimsies except in the Inverted Strawberry and Inverted Thistle patterns, but here is a rare green spittoon whimsey shaped from a tumbler. It is the only example reported and is very desirable. Cambridge called this pattern their #2699 Buzz Saw pattern but carnival collectors call it Double Star. It is the same pattern as the well-known Buzz Saw cruets.

A Dozen Roses

This rare footed bowl with stubby feet is a treasure in both design and color. It is believed to be made by Imperial and is found in amethyst, green, and marigold with few of each reported. The interior has 12 incised ovids and 12 raised flowers that somewhat resemble roses.

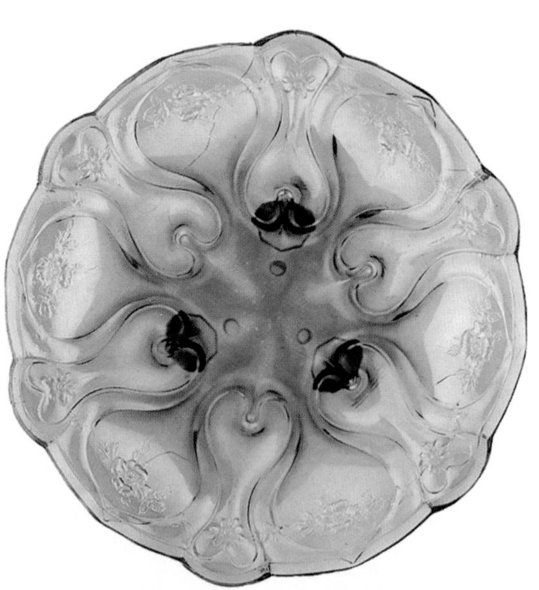

Dragon and Lotus Bowl

Made over several years and in many colors and treatments, this popular bowl shape is rare in aqua opalescent, vaseline opalescent, red, red opalescent, reverse amberina, or amethsyt opalescent. (It is rare in any color in plates.) Here is the ruffled bowl in a standout aqua opalescent treatment.

Dragon's Tongue

Dragon's Tongue from the Fenton Company is found on shades for lamps and very rare large bowls (10" – 11") shown. These bowls can be ruffled or ice cream shaped. The lamp shades are marigold-on-moonstone and match the design on the bowls nicely.

Drapery Rose Bowl (Northwood)

Like the Tree Trunk vase shown on page 193, this Northwood rose bowl is made of the very rare iridized blue slag glass. It is one of three reported pieces with such a treatment. The Drapery rose bowl can also be found in a rare Renninger blue glass. These two colors are some of the best in this pattern in either this shape or the candy dish from the same mould.

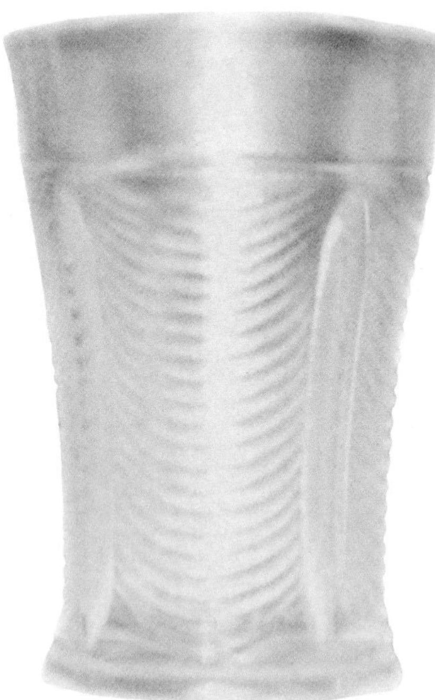

Drapery Tumbler (white)

This is one of two reported tumblers in this Northwood pattern. Both are white and seem to be a mystery since no water pitcher is known. There is also a small berry bowl in this color but no large berry bowls are known. At any rate, the tumblers are very desirable and expensive.

Dugan Elks Nappy

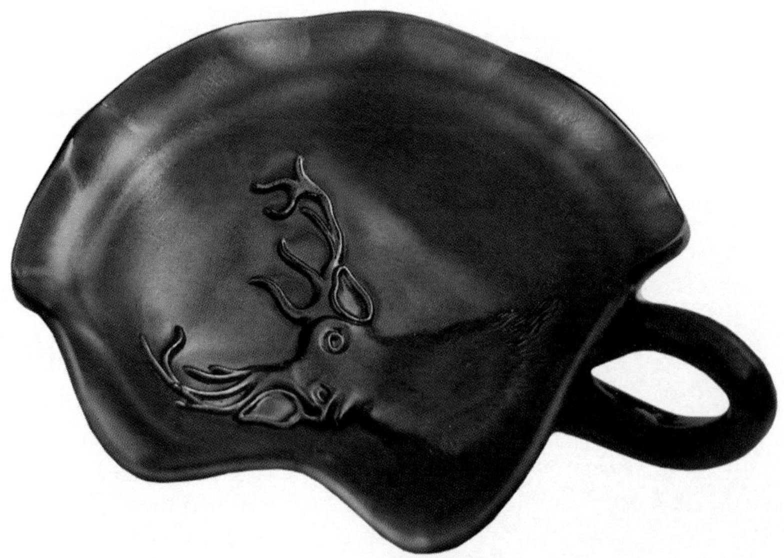

Like other carnival producers (Fenton, Northwood, Millersburg), the Dugan Company had a try at commemorative items. Rather plain compared to the Fenton or Millersburg Elks items, the Dugan nappy has only the elk's head as the interior design on a blank that had previously been used for both carnival and opalescent items that had a Leaf Ray design. Only four examples have been reported of the Elks nappy and we surmise the convention either didn't occur or the order was cancelled before production. At any rate all four nappies known are amethyst and all are spade shaped with a single ruffled example reported.

Durand Advertisement Bowl

This rare Fenton item is found only on a cobalt blue, footed orange bowl in the Grape and Cable pattern and is seldom discussed or sold. The advertising is raised in large letters on the marie's exterior and the inside of the bowl has the Persian Medallion pattern.

Eagle Furniture Company

This Northwood advertising piece is found in plates, hand-grip plates, and the double hand-grip plate as shown, with the Basketweave exterior. The lettering reads "Eagle Furniture Co. - 282-284 South Main Street." The business was in Memphis, Tennessee.

E.A. Hudson Furniture

This fine advertising item from the Northwood Company can be found in either a flat plate, a hand-grip plate, or a ruffled bowl (shown). The lettering says "E.A. Hudson Furniture Co. - 711 Travis St." We understand this company was in Houston, Texas. All pieces are amethyst.

Elegance

This very rare pattern is found on two marigold and one ice blue bowls and two ice blue plates. The pattern is busy but pleasing with rows of beading, triangles, stippling, floral sprays, and a center showing a multi-layered flower. The bowls measure 8¼" across and the plates almost 9". Northwood has been the suspected maker by some collectors but there certainly is no proof. At any rate, either color or shape is highly desirable.

Elks Bells

These Elks commemorative bells, from the Fenton Company, are found with three convention sites. Most of the relatively rare bells say either: "1911 - Atlantic City" or "1914 - Parkesburg," but one very rare bell showed up a few years ago that read "1912 - Portland." All these bells are on blue carnival glass, have a ringed handle, and show an elk's head superimposed on a clock.

Embroidered Mums Bowl

Embroidered Mums is one of Northwood's best-loved bowl and plate patterns. It was made in a host of colors including marigold, amethyst, cobalt blue, white, lavender, ice green, ice blue, aqua, aqua opalescent, ice blue opalescent, lime green opalescent, and sapphire. A ruffled bowl in aqua opalescent is shown.

Embroidered Mums Plate

Northwood certainly had good mould designers and this design shows their skills. Plates are found mostly in ice green but white (one known) and the cobalt blue shown (one known) exist and ice blue has long been rumored but never seen. In addition a rare white stemmed bonbon is known in this pattern.

Fancy Husk Corn Vase (Dugan)

This Dugan version of the corn vase is a beautiful thing. Only this single marigold piece is confirmed in carnival glass. It stands about 9" tall. This well known pattern is often found in opalescent glass or crystal. Just why it was made in carnival glass is a mystery. Fancy Husk vases have been reproduced in non-carnival treatments since the 1980s so be aware of examples with flat tops and solid husks.

Farmyard

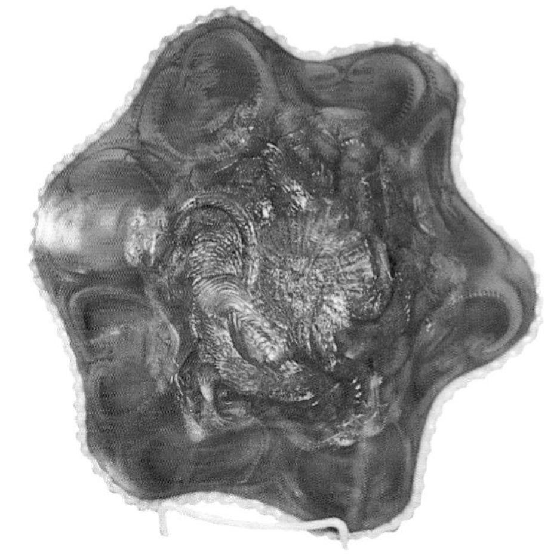

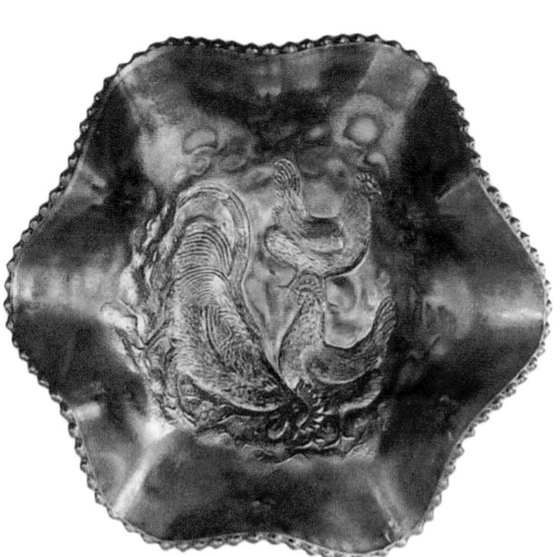

More desirable than rare, especially in ruffled amethyst bowls, this Dugan pattern has interesting rarities in shapes and colors. The six-ruffled bowl is found in a glorious peach opalescence (one known) and the three-in-one edged bowl is found in green. In addition there are the amethyst eight-ruffled bowls that can be squared (shown), square bowls with no ruffling (shown), and the very rare amethyst plate (one known and shown). And despite the bowl being reproduced in red, amethyst, and white (not from the original mould), the Farmyard pattern still stirs pulses and the prices remain high.

Fashion Rose Bowl

The Fashion Rose bowl can be found in marigold, helios green, and purple. It is the purple that causes all the excitement and well-iridized examples are expensive when sold. Fashion was Imperial's #402½ and was made in several shapes. It is one of the easiest patterns to find in marigold punch sets, but shapes in other colors are another story.

Feather and Heart Whimsey Hair Receiver (Millersburg)

This one-of-a-kind Millersburg rarity was shaped from a tumbler and has the top turned in to form a hair receiver shape. It is the only reported example and is a very desirable Millersburg whimsey.

Fenton Elks

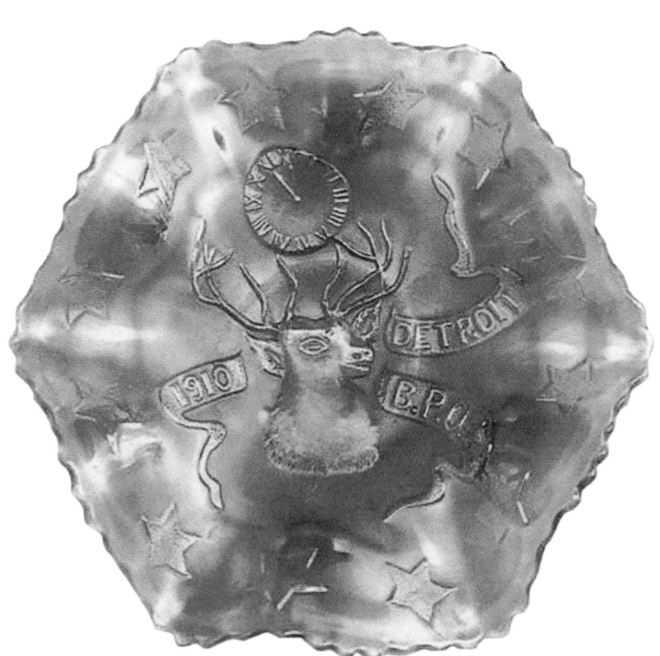

These bowls and plates (bells are covered elsewhere), carry a 1910 Detroit logo, a 1911 Atlantic City logo, and a 1914 Parkersburg logo. Bowls can be found in blue, amethyst, green, and a very rare marigold, and plates in blue or green.

Fenton Fine Rib Vase (vaseline opalescent)

Fenton's Fine Rib Vase is similar to the Northwood vase of the same name but the ribs end before the base flare. It is found in three base diameters and a host of colors including marigold, amethyst, green, blue, red, amberina, aqua, aqua opalescent, celeste blue, lime green opalescent, smoke, teal, marigold-over-moonstone, and the vaseline opalescent shown. Most colors are available but the red, moonstone, and vaseline opalescent are the big price pieces.

Fenton's Cherries

Seldom discussed and unknown to many collectors, this rare 9½" long footed banana boat from the Fenton Art Glass Company is very different from their other cherry patterns. In fact it looks more like the Millersburg Cherry design but isn't. There are four reported cobalt blue examples that have plain interiors, and at least one marigold example that is reported to have an interior design of flowers. All are rare and desirable. A close look at the cherries, leaves, and stems will reveal they match the exterior of the Mikado compote, also by Fenton.

Fern (Fenton)

This rare and mysterious pattern from the Fenton Art Glass Company is a real find. Only one blue 9" bowl and one clambroth 9" bowl have been reported. The example shown is nearly a plate shape with only the edges turned up. The design is a series of four web-like medallions that are each ringed by fern-like fronds. The iridescence is quite good and the pattern surely deserved more items to show off the design.

Fern Brand Chocolates

This Northwood advertising pattern is found in plates or hand-grip plates, has a fern frond above the lettering "Fern Brand Chocolates." Pieces are always the typical amethyst that is the most used glass color on these lettered items.

Fern Compote
(ice blue)

Fern is a very nice pattern from the Northwood Company that doesn't receive the attention it deserves. It is found on the interior of compotes with the Daisy and Plume pattern on the exterior. Colors are marigold, amethyst, or green, but here we show the first reported ice blue example and it gives this compote a whole new look. Please note how the stem is twisted.

Field-Flower Pitcher

Why Imperial chose to use this beautiful pattern on only a tumbler, a milk pitcher, and a water pitcher is a mystery. The tumbler can be found in blue, green, red, violet, amber, or marigold. The milk pitcher is found in clambroth and marigold. The water pitcher (shown here) is found in green, amber, blue, smoke, or marigold. Most items are rather rare with the red tumbler and the smoke pitcher the hardest to find.

Filigree Vase

Apparently dating from 1909 at the beginning of Dugan's production of iridized glass, the Filigree vase is the only known piece of carnival in this pattern, and may well have been a prototype piece. The Filigree pattern dates to 1907 and is well known in other types of glass that include custard, gilded, and colored glass. The vase is mould blown and has a typical Art Nouveau pattern of scrolling and gothic arches and panels. The color is a bronzy amethyst and the iridescence is rich with blues and golds.

Fisherman's Mug

Apparently spanning the time from Dugan production to Diamond, this mug, despite being reproduced in custard glass, has become a collectors' favorite. It is found mostly in amethyst, but marigold, cobalt blue, and lavender are known. The real rarity is the peach opalescent mug shown and these bring a top price when offered.

Fleur-de-Lis Compote

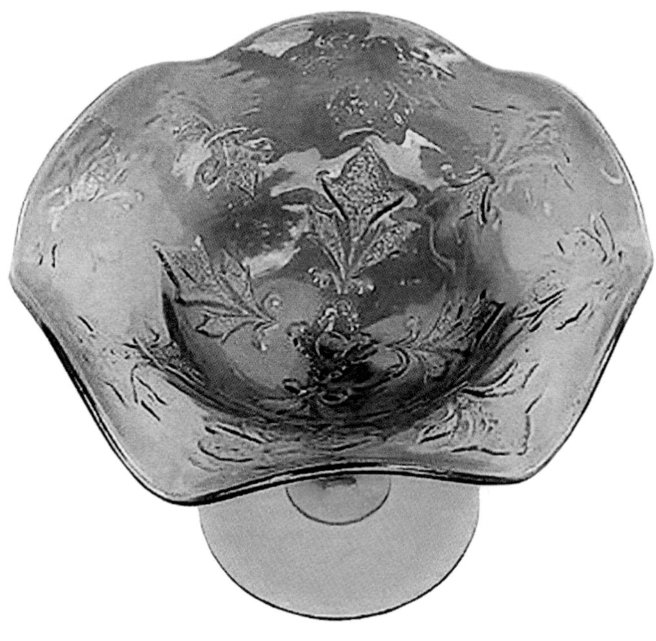

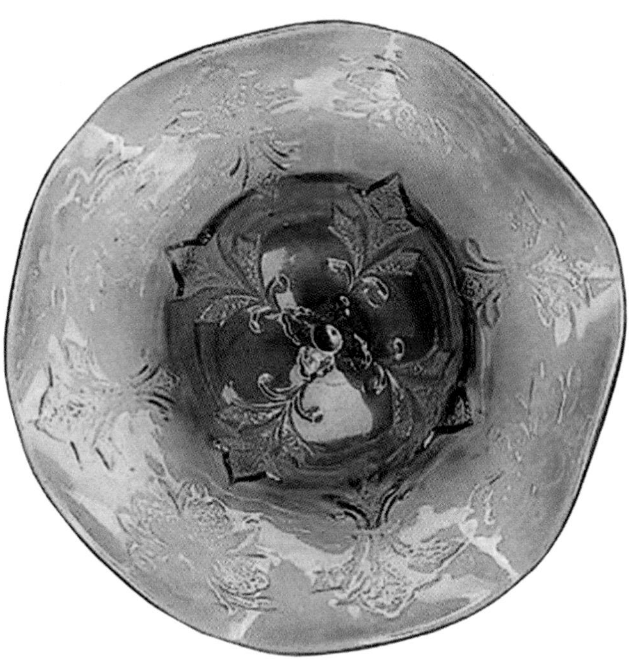

When this extreme rarity was first reported, it was as if all of the Millersburg collectors had been waiting for just such a new revelation. It is the only one of its kind to be reported in any color, so just why it even exists is a mystery. The stem is very different from other Millersburg compote stems and is only found on a mould drawing that most of us had believed was never put into production.

Fleur-de-Lis Rose Bowl

This is a well-balanced pattern from Millersburg that is found on collar-based bowls or dome-based bowls in marigold, amethyst, green, or vaseline (rare). Some bowls are shaped into rose bowls (both collar or dome) and some are shaped into tri-corner pieces. Presently only two or three examples in each rose bowl shape are known and all are amethyst.

Floral and Grape Variant Vase

This basic pattern was made by both Dugan and Fenton. This vase whimsey, from the pitcher mould, was made by Fenton around 1911. The handle has been left off and the top flared widely. The color is cobalt blue with outstanding iridescence. Only this single example has been reported, making it quite rare and very collectible.

Flowering Vine

This was made by Millersburg from the same mould as the Rosalind compote. The Flowering Vine shows an interior of Dahlia-type flowers and leaves that winds around the bowl with a large center flower. The only examples reported are two amethyst, one green, and one marigold. Seldom sold, this 9" tall beauty is a well designed rarity and deserves the lofty position it holds in the compote world.

Frolicking Bears

Collectors of carnival glass do not have to be told how rare and important this water set is. It is believed to have been made by U.S. Glass (crystal tumblers exist). In carnival glass only the olive green glass with irdescence is known. Both the very rare pitcher and the equally rare tumblers have an abbreviated dome base with scalloped edges. The bears appear in various poses before a background of moutains and vining grapes and leaves meander around the top and bottom of each piece.

Fruit Basket

This Millersburg two-handled, footed bonbon is made from the same mould as their Roses and Fruit, but the interior has been changed to show a basketweave background with a cluster of fruit (pineapple, grapes, cherries, apples, etc.) in the bottom. Only a few of these are known (five or six) and all are amethyst; they seldom come up for sale and are very desirable.

Fruit Salad Punch Set

This is found only in the punch set shown, in marigold, amethyst, peach opalescent (shown), and a very rare blue opalescent (no cups are reported). It is unique in shape with the raised points around the rim. The design shows pineapples, cherries, apples, and grapes. All pieces are considered rare with peach opalescent ones and the single blue opalescent bowl and base the rarest.

Fruits and Flowers

Fruits and Flowers was made by Northwood in a stemmed bonbon, bowls (5" – 10"), plates (7" – 9"), and a handgrip plate. Colors are many but the pastels are the rarest. Here is a rare ice green 9½" bowl (it was photographed on black and looks darker) with a Basketweave exterior. The iridescence is very blue giving the piece a fantastic look.

Garden Path Variant Chop Plate

Just why Dugan made two versions of this design is a puzzle, but they did. The most spectacular pieces are the large 11" chop plates. Colors are marigold, amethyst, and peach opalescent. Dugan's Soda Gold pattern is on the exterior and this is a good combination, especially on the peach opalescent pieces where both designs show through.

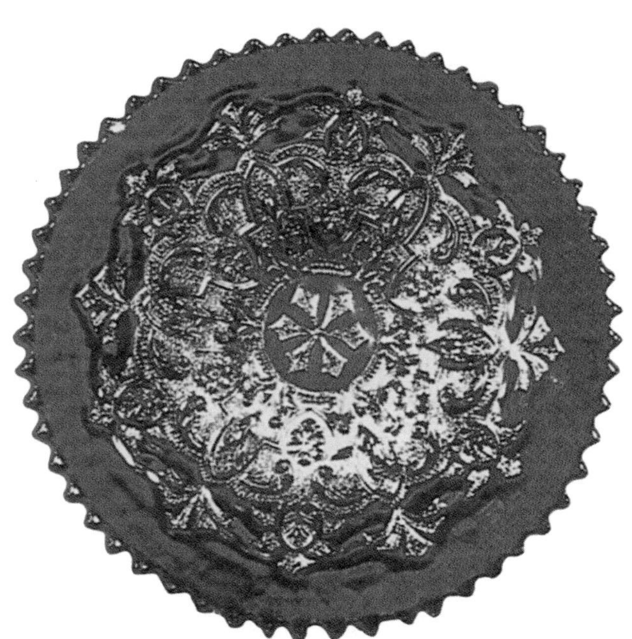

Gay 90s Water Set

Another Millersburg gem, this water set ranks very high on both the rarity and the desirability list. The pitchers are found in amethyst (four) and green (one), and tumblers are found in amethyst, marigold (three), and the single green one shown. The design is very similar to Millersburg's Rosalind pattern in many ways with rows of overlapping festoons and a scroll above.

Geo. W. Getts

This is one of Fenton's advertising pieces that is found in ice cream shaped bowls, ruffled bowls, and plates. All are amethyst and the lettering reads "Geo. W. Getz, Pianos, Grand Forks (please note the "s" is backwards in Forks), N. Dak."

Gevurtz Brothers

This advertising piece was made by Fenton in bowls, flat plates, and hand-grip plates. It reads "Gevurtz Bros. – Furniture & Clothing – Union Ave & East Brunside St.," a Portland, Oregon, firm. All pieces are amethyst and bring an average price for these advertising pieces.

God and Home

Despite all the reproductions of this very fine water set, the old pieces still bring a good price and are collectors' favorites. It is believed this set came from either Dugan or Diamond. Old pieces are only known in cobalt blue; new examples are found in cobalt blue, amethyst, red, ice green, and a host of uniridized items in slag. Old God and Home water sets are quite rare.

Goddess of Harvest

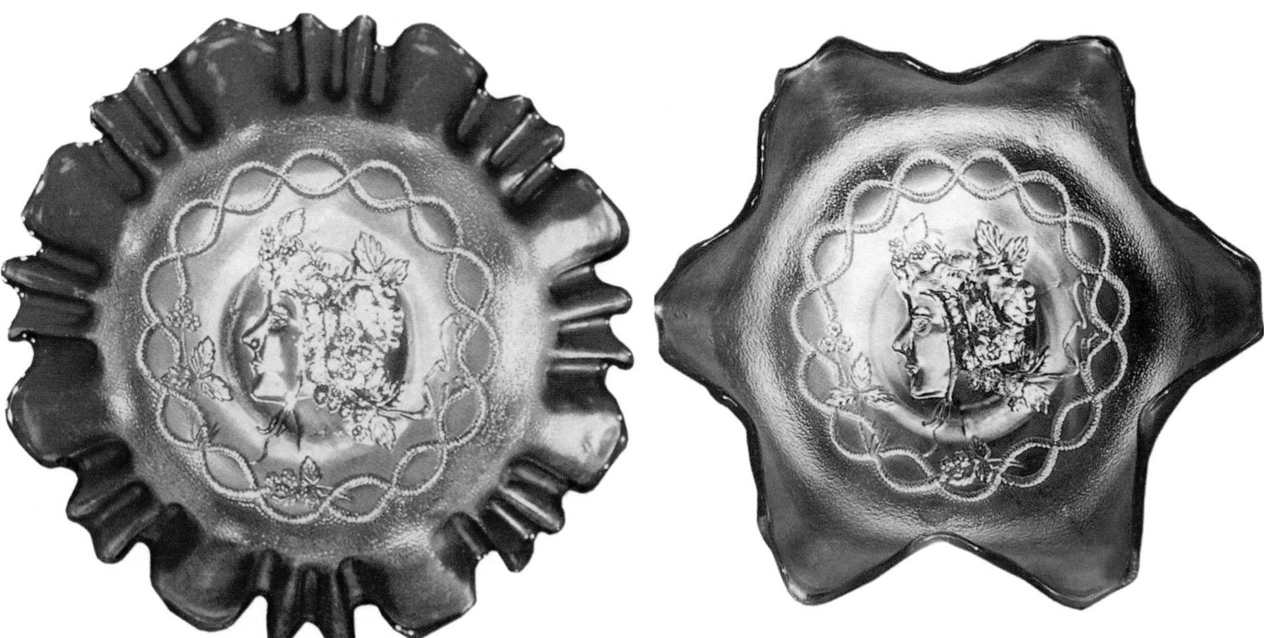

According to Nellie Glasco in 1980 (she was John Fenton's daughter), this bowl was designed by her father and depicts her mother. Whether this is the case or not, we can't confirm, but the bowl pattern from the Fenton Art Glass Company is very rare. It is found in ice cream, ruffled, a three-in-one edge, or tightly crimped bowls and ultra-rare plates (two known). Bowls are known in marigold, amethyst, and blue, and plates in amethyst.

Good Luck Bowl

The well known Good Luck is high on the list of favorite bowl patterns by Northwood. It was made in many colors in plates as well as bowls, and there are some mould variations too. The ruffled bowl is shown in aqua opalescent glass, which along with ice green and white, is one of the most desired colors. One has to wonder if Harry Northwood had any idea of how popular this color would be?

Good Luck Bowl (ice blue)

This beautiful ice blue, eight-ruffled bowl with a rib exterior is what pastels are all about. Only ice green and ice blue opalescent are rarer. No wonder collectors are eager to add these to their collections and that they sell for high prices.

Good Luck Enameled Bowl

When rarity meets a beautiful treatment of glass, the result has to be exciting, and this Northwood bowl is instant proof. It is a cobalt blue Good Luck bowl with electric iridescence but the real treat is the one-of-a-kind enameling of the flowers, leaves, and wheat stems on the bowl. The horseshoe and stems of wheat are gilded and the small berries are red while the flowers are yellow and white and the leaves are green. The enameling was done before the iridescence was applied.

Good Luck Plate (electric purple)

The plates are much scarcer than bowls in this pattern. They were made only in marigold, amethyst, green, cobalt blue, ice blue, ice green, and horehound. Shown is a non-stippled plate in amethyst (not a rare color at all) but look at the iridescence! It is a blast of colors called "electric" and adds to the collector's interest.

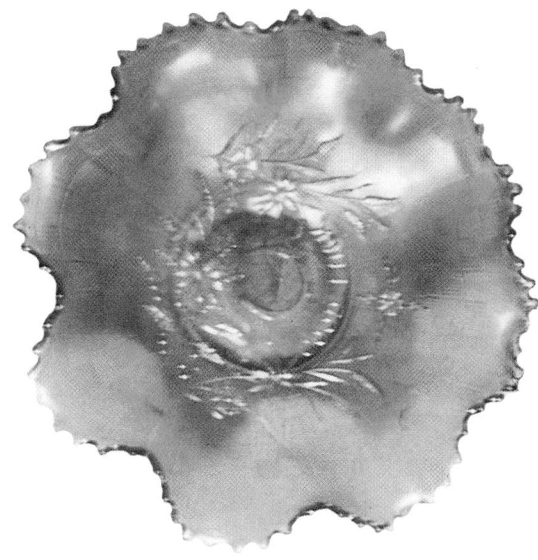

Good Luck Prototype Bowl

Just why the Northwood Company chose to make this pattern in stages is a mystery but they certainly did. The bowl shown here is the very first stage with a minimum of design clustered in the bowl's center. Three bowls with this work are known. One is ice cream shaped while the other two are ruffled. The exterior carries the Basketweave pattern.

Grape and Cable Banquet-Sized Punch Set (ice blue)

This prolific Northwood pattern has three sizes in the punch set (small, mid-size, and the large master or banquet set) shown. Rare in ice green, this set is extremely rare in the ice blue shown and only the aqua opalescent set in the small size rates above the ice blue in desirability. To date, only this one example has been reported and it stands 18½" tall and measures 17" across the top of the bowl.

Grape and Cable Bonbon (peach opalescent)

As part of Northwood's gigantic line in this pattern, it is hard to see why more of these rare bonbons in this color haven't been found but to this time only two or three examples are known. This piece is peach opalescent (examples are also known in iridized cusard glass), has a plain background, and there are examples with a stippled background but not in this color.

Grape and Cable Bride's Basket

Actually this is the large orange bowl or fruit bowl to which a hand-shaped handle has been applied. The interior is plain and the iridescence is spectacular. At this time three examples are reported: two in amethyst and the single blue shown. The maker is the Fenton Art Glass Company.

Grape and Cable
Cologne Whimsies

These two outstanding whimsies were fashioned from the Northwood cologne bottles in their famous Grape and Cable pattern. The first is an oil lamp made by pinching in the neck and adding a burner when the glass was hot; and the second is a vase shaped by widening the cologne's neck and pulling it down on three sides. Both pieces are reported to be one-of-a-kind whimsies at this time and are very rare and desirable.

Grape and Cable Covered Compote

This Northwood covered compote is readily found in amethyst with a bit of a search but the marigold shown is a different affair. It is massive, rare, and very desirable, making it a real favorite of Grape and Cable collectors.

Grape and Cable Cracker Jar (aqua opalescent)

This seldom discussed Northwood covered cracker (or cookie) jar with matching lid has two handles and stands about 8" tall to the tip of the finial. It is easily available in amethyst or marigold but rather rare in blue, ice green, white, and smoke. The aqua opalescent shown takes rarity to a new level in this shape with three or four known (some are missing the lid), and unless they are sold privately, they never seem to be traded.

Grape and Cable Fernery

This Northwood large footed piece is round with steep straight sides. It is hard to find in any color but especially white, ice blue, or ice green. Other colors that bring less are marigold, amethyst, or pearlized custard.

Grape and Cable Hatpin Holder (aqua opalescent)

We understand there are fewer than a half-dozen Grape and Cable hatpin holders in aqua opalescent known, making this a truly rare group (some are damaged). Just what makes this treatment so desirable is easy to see; it just grabs you. Add to that the short production span and its rarity on most items and you can understand why we are showing so much of it in this book.

Grape and Cable Humidor Spittoon

Pulled and shaped from the base of the Northwood Grape and Cable humidor, this rare, one-of-a-kind item is a collector's dream. It is 4¾" tall, has a 5¼" base diameter, and measures 7" across the top. The coloring is a strong pumpkin marigold with very good iridescence. Strangely, this rare item was only discovered in 1998 and one has to wonder why nobody had heard of its existence before that time.

Grape and Cable Powder Jar

This covered powder jar was made as part of Northwood's dresser set or sold separately. It is found in marigold, amethyst, green, cobalt blue (rare), lavender, and the rare ice green, white, and ice blue. The aqua opalescent example shown here (one of two known) is in a class by itself and is a standout in any collection.

Grape and Cable Punch Set
(aqua opalescent)

Undoubtedly the premier punch set in all of carnival glass, this very rare and expensive grouping brought the top price for carnival glass when it was purchased in 1996. For years, rumors of such a set in this well-loved color were heard and indeed cups were known, but to put the whole set together was a major accomplishment for the owners. Aqua opalescent carnival glass is achieved by iridizing aqua or ice blue glass with a marigold treatment, giving one of the most prized colors in all of carnival glass. Only Northwood, Fenton, and Millersburg (two vases) tried this coloring with most examples being made by Northwood from 1912 to 1915.

Grape and Cable Small Spittoon

Unlike the larger piece that was shaped from a humidor bottom, the small spittoon whimsey was made from the base of the covered powder jar. Found in marigold, amethyst, or green (only three green examples reported and a handful in each of the other colors), this cutie is very cherished by the few who are fortunate to own one.

Grape and Cable Vase Whimsey

This vase whimsey was shaped from the familiar Grape and Cable hatpin holder by Northwood. It has the top flared out in small points rather than the usual larger turned-in ones. These are known in amethyst or green but either color is extremely rare and very coveted by collectors.

Grape and Cable with Thumbprint Standard Pitcher

A comparison of this pitcher and the tankard one shown elsewhere will give the reader some idea of the variety in this Northwood pattern. The standard pitcher is about 8½" tall while the tankard is two inches more. Found mostly in amethyst or marigold, the standard size can also be found in green, a very rare smoke, and the very rare ice green shown.

Grape and Cable with Thumbprint Tankard Pitcher

While this tall pitcher is rare in any color, the green and ice green are ultra-rare. As a part of Northwood's vast grape design line, this beauty stands about 11" tall and has the thumbprints around the base. The grapes and leaves stand out in high relief, hanging from the finely detailed cable.

Grape Arbor

The tankard pitcher in this a stately water set from Northwood is mould-blown and is really a wonder. Hat whimsies, pulled from the tumbler, are known in marigold, blue, ice green, and white, while the tumblers are seen in marigold, amethyst, lavender, blue, ice green, ice blue, white, iridized custard, and aqua. The pitchers are found in marigold, amethyst, white, ice blue, blue (shown), and the very rare ice green shown.

Grape Leaves
(Millersburg)

Grape Leaves is a seldom seen and little discussed pattern from Millersburg with the wonderful Mayflower exterior. It is found only on bowls in marigold, amethyst, green, and the single vaseline one shown. The pattern is distinguished by a single cluster of grapes in the center with four leaves around it, while grapes, leaves, and vines wind around the middle of the bowl.

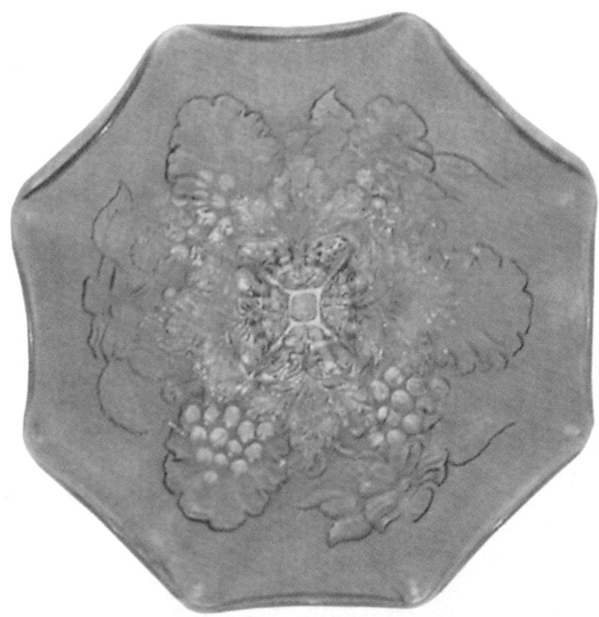

Grape Leaves Bowl (ice blue)

This nicely done Northwood bowl is a carnival favorite. Bowls are about 8½" and are found in marigold, amethyst, green, cobalt blue, clambroth, amber, lavender, and the rare ice blue shown. Marigold and amethyst are easily found and create little interest. Green is scarce and cobalt blue, amber, and clambroth are really rare, but all take back seat to the ice blue shown.

Greek Key Bowl (Renninger blue)

Not as prolific in colors or as much in demand as some Northwood patterns, this beautiful design is found in water sets, dome-base bowls, collar-based bowls, and a 9" plate. Colors for the bowls are marigold, amethyst, green, cobalt blue, and ice green, but here is one in Renninger blue. It has a ribbed back and is eight-ruffled.

Greek Key Pitcher

Well designed, this is one of Northwood's best patterns. It is found in bowls, plates, and water sets. Bowls may have a collar base or be dome based. The very desirable water sets are known in marigold, amethyst, or green, and usually have outstanding iridescence like the one shown.

Greengard Furniture

One of Millersburg's very rare advertising patterns, Greengard Furniture is known in a single ruffled bowl, a handgrip plate (one known), and three double handgrip plates (shown). The lettering reads "Greengard Furniture Co. – 11020 Mich. Ave. – Roseland, Ill." The mould is the same as the Campbell and Beesley piece shown elsewhere.

Hattie Chop Plate

This amber 11" chop plate is a fantastic item and deserves all the praise it receives. It can also be seen in marigold, purple, green, or clambroth. The Hattie design is from Imperial Glass and is also found on bowls and a rare rose bowl, but the plates seem to get the raves. Hattie is one of those straight designs that is duplicated on the exterior as well as the interior.

Hearts and Flowers (vaseline plate)

While this Northwood pattern was made in many colors in both bowls and plates, it is the vaseline plate which holds top honors as to rarity and desirability. Only two are known and we understand both have some slight damage but that doesn't undermine their value to collectors. These plates are 9" in diameter and have the Thin Rib exterior, one of Northwood's standard exterior designs.

Heavy Iris Pitcher (white)

Heavy Iris is one of the Dugan Glass Company's better water set designs. The pitcher is mould blown and can be found with a ruffled rim as shown or a straight rim (one example in white is known). Colors are marigold, amethyst, white, and peach opalescent (one pitcher reported). Heavy Iris has been reproduced from the original moulds and sold by L.G. Wright, so be cautious.

Heavy Pineapple

This quite rare and little discussed pattern is from Fenton and can be found in large bowls, either collar based or footed as shown. Colors are marigold, cobalt blue, or white with less than a dozen examples known in all colors. The design is well done with pineapples, vines, and leaf fans making it quite distinctive.

Heavy Web Chop Plate

This magnificent chop plate by Dugan is the only reported example in this shape in the Heavy Web pattern. It has the grape cluster exterior (some bowls have a morning glory design on the outside), and it measures about 11" across. The coloring is peach opalescent as are all pieces found in this pattern thus far.

Hobnail Pitcher

This rare Millersburg pattern is found in a table set, a water set, and a rose bowl as well as the rare spittoon shown elsewhere. The pitcher shown is found in marigold, amethyst, blue, and green, with the latter being the rarest. The table set can be found in the same colors but no blue is known in the rose bowl. And there is a rare hat whimsey pulled from a tumbler, known in marigold only.

Hobnail Spittoon (green)

This pattern is from the Millersburg Hobnail group that consists of water sets, table sets, vases, rose bowls, and spittoons (the latter two from the same mould), and is very similar to their Swirl Hobnail pattern. Spittoons are known in marigold, amethyst, and the green shown. It is this green that is the jewel of colors; it is very rare and very desirable.

Hobnail Table Set (Millersburg)

Like the Hobnail pitcher and the spittoon whimsey, this table set is a great rarity and about as complete as most sets get, with only the spooner missing. Table set pieces are found in amethyst, marigold, green, and blue. Amethyst may be a bit more plentiful than marigold. It is almost impossible to put the four pieces together to complete a set in green or blue.

Hobnail Variant

This very rare pattern is of questionable origin (most of us feel this is Millersburg). It is known only in the two shapes shown, a rose bowl and a jardiniere that resembles a nut bowl. The rose bowl is reported only in marigold while the jardiniere is found in both amethyst and a very rare blue. The finish on both shapes is a fine radium and the glass is clear and sparkling.

Hobstar and Feather Bridge Set Pieces

All four shapes (heart, diamond, spade, club) are known in crystal, and a few rare pieces are known in ruby stained glass (club and spade only). In carnival glass, only the heart and diamond shapes have been reported and both are very hard to find, especially the diamond.

Hobstar and Feather Giant Compote (flared)

This beautiful flared compote is shaped from the giant rose bowl mould, just like the vase whimsey, spittoon whimsey, and ruffled compote. It is sometimes called a one piece punchbowl by some collectors. It is, of course, a Millersburg product and at this time one green, one amethyst, and one crystal piece (not iridized) are known, and all are rare and treasured by their owners.

Hobstar and Feather Giant Compote (ruffled)

Like the flared version of this rare Millersburg piece, this one-of-a-kind giant compote is fashioned from the giant rose bowl mould. It has only come to light in the last two years. It is a beautiful color with heavy satin finish. It currently belongs to a well known Millersburg area collector and has to be a treasured part of his glass.

Hobstar and Feather Punch Set

This punch set is found in marigold (mostly), amethyst (a lot rarer), and green (only bits and pieces that include bowls and cups). Both the green and the marigold can be found with the Fleur-de-lis interior or plain and only the amethyst has thus far been found in the beautiful tulip shape with the top turned in (shown). All pieces are on very thick glass and are massive in concept, making them standouts in any collection.

Hobstar and Feather Sauce

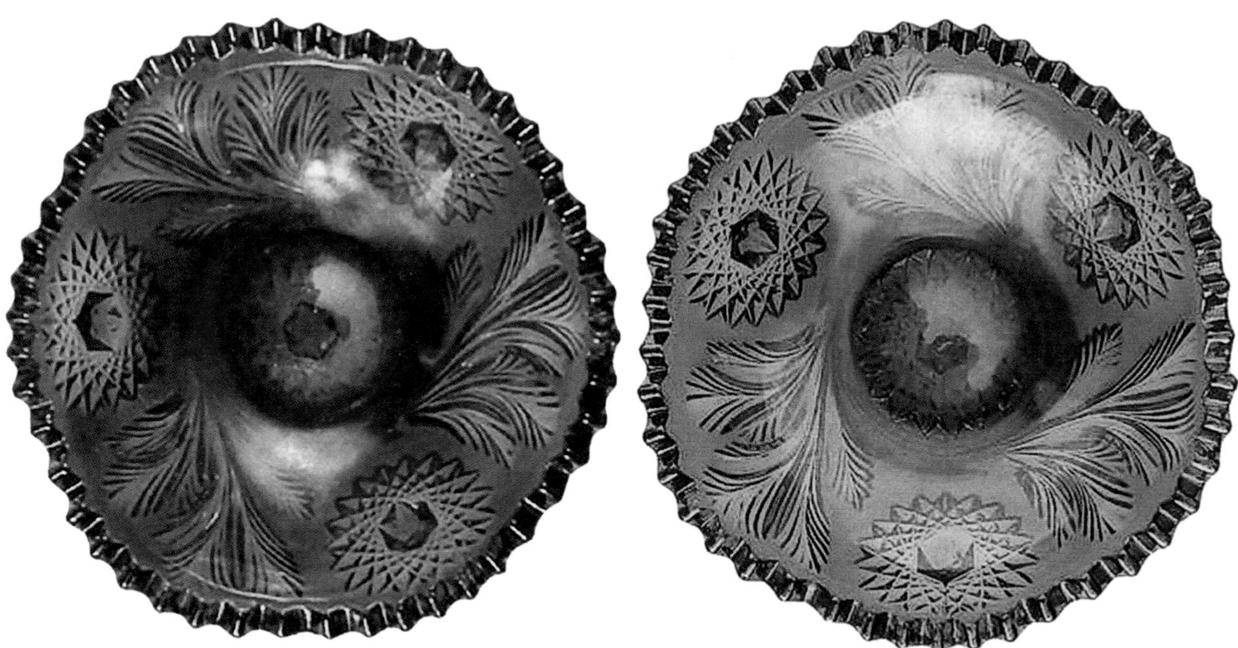

This extremely rare sauce, one of Millersburg's best patterns (or anyone else's), is a standout. Until recently only a handful of amethyst examples existed and these are considered rare and quite desirable. The green one is in a class by itself and can only be described by Millersburg collectors as a top attraction. It is a real pleasure to include it in this book of rare and desirable glass.

Hobstar and Feather Spittoon Whimsey

This rare Millersburg whimsey is a massive masterpiece formed from the wonderful giant rose bowl mould. It is found in amethyst and is the only reported example in this shape despite at least three other whimsey shapes from this mould (a flared compote, a ruffled compote, and a vase, all shown in this book).

Hobstar and Feather Table Set Pieces

You can't say enough about the beauty of this pattern and its rarity in table set pieces. Three covered butter dishes are known in amethyst, one each of the creamer is known in amethyst and green, two amethyst and one green covered sugars are known, and one amethyst, one green, one marigold, and two vaseline spooners are known. And on each and every example we've seen, the radium finish was fantastic, just like the examples shown.

Hobstar and Feather Vase

This beautiful and massive vase is swung or pulled from the giant rose bowl from Millersburg. It is known in both amethyst (two confirmed) and green (two confirmed). The example shown is about 16" tall and weighs over five pounds! The glass is very thick and the design is deeply tooled. These vases very seldom change owners and seem to only come out for carnival glass convention displays so anyone owning one is very fortunate indeed. It is pleasure just to see one.

Holly (Fenton)

Fenton's Holly pattern is a very prolific one, found in bowls of several shapes, plates, rose bowls, hats, and compotes. Colors are many but red, vaseline, ice green, ice blue, or celeste blue probably create the most stir except for marigold-over-moonstone, aqua opalescent, or blue opalescent. Here is a 9" ruffled bowl in red that isn't too difficult to find but still is desirable and brings a hefty price.

Holly and Poinsettia

Despite there being no solid confirmation, most collectors feel this rare (only the single example shown has ever been found) dome-based compote is from the Dugan Glass Company. A comparison with Dugan's Christmas compote shows strong similarities between the two. The coloring is a strong marigold and the pattern a nicely done wreath of leaves and berries that circle the compote from just above the base to the rim. The poinsettia flowers nestle nicely among the leaves and vine in a random pattern.

Holly Bowl

This example, shown on one of the most found patterns in carnival glass, has a three-in-one edge and is a marigold iridescence on milk glass. It is rare and only the second example reported with this edge and on this treatment.

Holly Bowl (marigold-on-moonstone)

This very rare Fenton bowl is marigold-on-moonstone and is a sight to behold. This same bowl can be found in an eight-ruffled bowl but this is the only one reported with a three-in-one edge. It elevates this common Fenton pattern to the extraordinary.

Holly Plate (black amethyst)

This is one of the rarest colors in this pattern, especially on the 9½ " plate shown. It seems to hold iridescence in a special way that lights up the surface, showing a lot of green, gold, and red. Northwood, Fenton, and Dugan all used this color for carnival glass and most pieces are very well done.

Holly Sprig Compote
(Millersburg)

At first glance, this may be mistaken for the Strawberry Wreath compotes, made on the same mould, but this very rare Holly design is a much different thing. Three marigold and two amethyst are reported and there have long been rumors of a vaseline one but no evidence. The Millersburg coloring is superb and the radium finish about as good as it gets. The compote shown has four ruffles, turning it into a square shape.

Honeycomb and Hobstar

Honeycomb and Hobstar was originally made by the Ohio Flint Glass Company in crystal and ruby stained crystal, in 1906. When that company closed in 1907, the moulds went to Jefferson Glass and in 1909 the mould for this vase shape was purchased by John Fenton for the Millersburg Glass Company. The vase stands 8¼ " tall on a pedestal base and has alternating rows of hobstars and sunken honeycomb. It is both rare and desirable, with two amethyst and two blue examples currently reported. Ohio Flint originally called this their Gloria pattern.

Horse's Head

Also called Horse Medallion, this Fenton pattern is very popular. It can be found in flat bowls, footed bowls, a plate shape, a nut bowl shape, and the footed rose bowl. The color range is wide, but the rarest piece of all is the example shown, a red rose bowl. Other rare colors include aqua, vaseline, and green, or amethyst in plates.

Idyll Vase

One of the Fenton Art Glass Company's hidden treasures, this 7" vase is really a variation of their Waterlilly and Cattails pattern with an added Butterfly. It is found in chocolate glass as well as the carnival colors of marigold, amethyst (shown), and cobalt blue. All are extremely rare.

Illinois Soldiers and Sailors Plate

Not as rare as most items in this book but still very desirable, these plates, shown in marigold and cobalt blue, are from Fenton and have their well-known Berry and Leaf Circle exterior. They measure 7½" across and commemorate the soldier's and sailor's home in Quincy, Illinois.

Indiana Soldiers and Sailors Plate

This Fenton commemorative piece with the Berry and Leaf Circle exterior can be found in bowls and plates, but only rarely. It shows the Indiana Soldiers and Sailors Monument in Monument Circle in downtown Indianapolis that was erected as a Civil Ware memorial. The lettering says "Soldiers and Sailors Monument - Indianapolis, Ind." All pieces are cobalt blue.

Indiana Statehouse

This is a companion piece to the Indiana Soldiers and Sailors pieces, also from Fenton. It has the same exterior pattern of Berry and Leaf Circle, but can be found in rare marigold plates as well as cobalt blue. The design shows the old Indiana Statehouse and is lettered "State House of Indiana." Presently, three or four blue and two marigold have been reported.

Inverted Feather Punch Set

Besides the green example shown (two known), there are two or three marigold sets (one badly damaged) and a few odd cups and bases in this pattern. Seldom do sets in either color come to market and most sales in the last three decades have been private so it is hard to determine who owns them. Like most Cambridge glass, the design is very well done and many pieces will have the Cambridge "Near Cut" mark.

Inverted Feather Tankard Water Set

Cambridge listed this pattern as their #2651 and in crystal it was made in a host of shapes. In carnival glass the most often seen pieces are a covered cracker jar and a compote or stemmed sherbet glass. In addition there are scarce items like a covered powder jar and a table set, and rarer items include a squat water pitcher and a very rare punch set. Equally as rare is the tankard water set shown. It is known in marigold and the very rare amethyst. It is a collector's dream, showing all the quality Cambridge put into their carnival in the brief time they made iridized glass.

Inverted Strawberry Spittoon

Found in marigold, green, and amethyst, this small spittoon was made from a small bowl mould and is a highly prized item with collectors. The design is very good and all intaglio, or recessed. And despite being made in some quantity, they sell for fairly large amounts for such a small item.

Inverted Strawberry Water Set

This fabulous pattern is a real eye-popper and the tall stately water set bears that out. It is found in marigold, green, and the amethyst shown, but in very limited amounts of each. In addition there is a rare milk pitcher in amethyst and a handful of novelty or whimsey items that are very desirable. Certain shapes were reproduced in the 1970s.

Inverted Thistle Milk Pitcher

Cambridge made this rare pattern mostly in crystal or decorated crystal, but it is found in iridized glass in berry sets, table sets, water sets, a compote, a chop plate, a covered box, and the green milk pitcher shown. Colors for most pieces are either amethyst or green.

Jockey Club

As far-fetched as it may seem, this advertising piece by the Northwood Company has nothing to do with horses or racing — it supposedly represents a California perfume company! It is found on ruffled bowls, plates, and hand-grip plates. The exterior is Northwood's Basketweave pattern and the usual color is amethyst but here we show a very rare pale lavender plate.

Lattice and Grape Spittoon

This spittoon was fashioned from a Lattice and Grape tumbler in marigold. It is a top Fenton whimsey and the only example reported. It has been in the same collection for decades.

Leaf Chain Plate (ice green)

Shown is a 7½" plate in Fenton's Leaf Chain design. This was their #1416 pattern and is found on bowls and plates in two sizes. This is the first example reported in the rare ice green, and is a top rarity in this pattern.

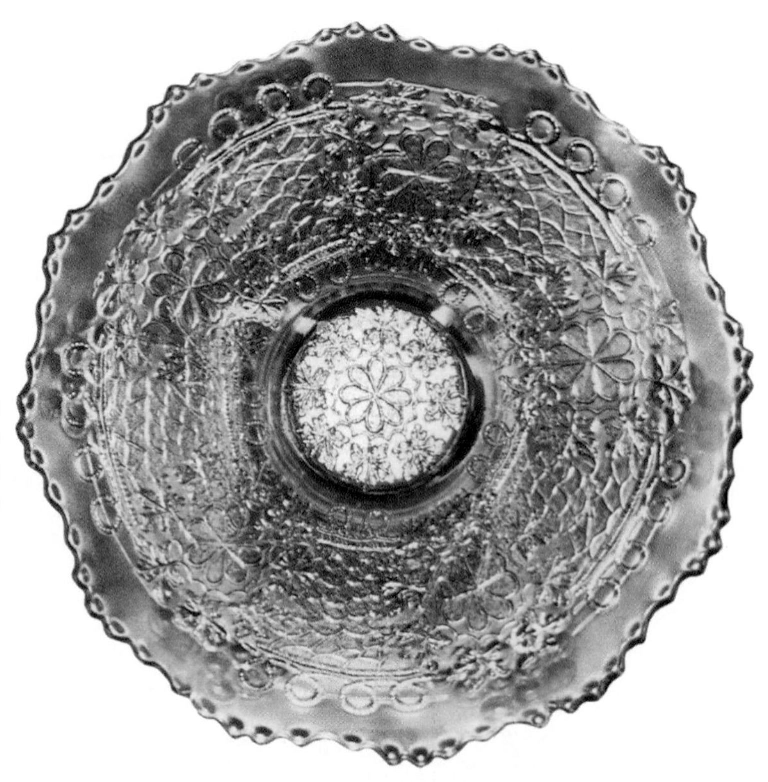

Leaf Tiers Master Bowl (blue)

Leaf Tiers, Fenton's #1790 pattern, is also called Stippled Leaf. It is found in opalescent glass, opaque glass, and a few items in carnival glass including a water set, table set, light shade, and a footed berry set. Most all are marigold or marigold-on-milk glass, but the water set is found in green, blue, and amethyst as well. The berry set has previously been reported in marigold only but here is the master bowl in cobalt blue. It is shaped like a centerpiece and is very rare.

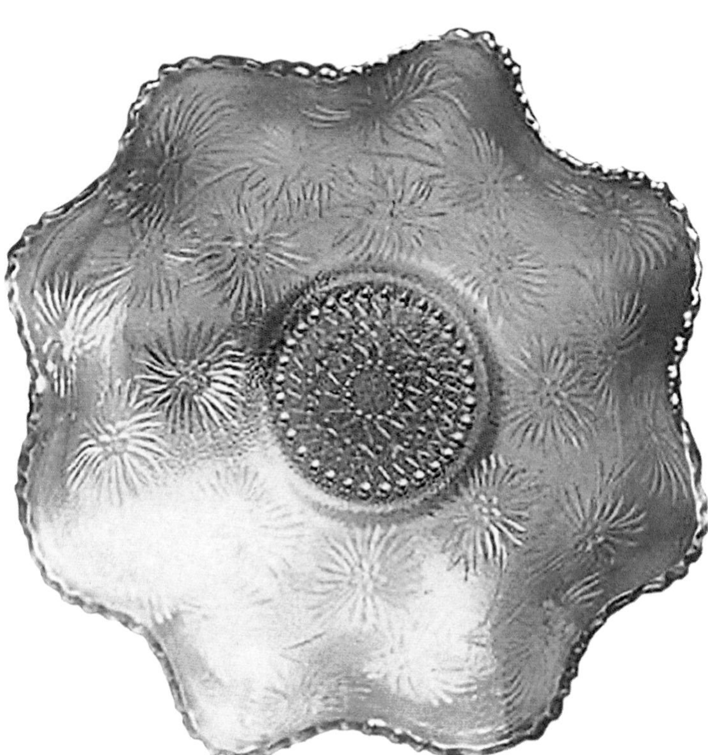

Little Daisies

Little Daisies, from the Fenton Art Glass Company, is found on bowls that measure 9" to 10". Bowls can be ruffled or straight sided. The colors are marigold and cobalt blue, and the design is one of flowers bursting like stars with an interior marie design of beads and zigzagging. These rare bowls have no exterior pattern. They continue to be a favorite whenever they come up for sale.

Lily of the Valley

As part of one of Fenton's more beautiful water sets, this tall and regal pitcher was first made in 1912. This water pitcher's pattern is unique and develops over three sections. It is found only in blue, although at one time a very rare marigold pitcher is said to have existed but was destroyed in a California quake. Marigold tumblers do exist but are also very rare.

Linn's Mums

Linn's Mums, made by Northwood, is also known as Dancing Daisies. The exterior carries the Ruffles and Rings pattern Northwood purchased from Jefferson Glass. This pretty and rare bowl has scroll feet. The flowers are much like those found on several of Northwood's advertising bowls and plates may have been tooled by the same designer. There are two examples known and both are amethyst.

Lion Plate

This pattern, from the Fenton Art Glass Company, can be found in ruffled, ice cream, or deeper and round bowls that measure 6" to 7" across or marigold plates that measure 7" to 8". Bowls are found in both marigold and cobalt blue and are reported in a rare powder blue.

Little Fishes Low ICS Bowl

What a great shape this shallow ice cream bowl is. The pattern is Fenton's Little Fishes. This large, footed bowl is cobalt blue. Next to the reported chop plate, this piece has to be at the top of this pattern's rare and desirable list and would cause a sensation in any collection.

Little Flowers Bowl (red)

Little Flowers was made by Fenton in berry sets, ruffled bowls, ice cream bowls, 7" plates, and a 10" chop plate. The rare colors are amberina and red (shown). The chop plate is very desirable in marigold.

Little Stars

Blue has always been a rare color for Millersburg glass in any pattern and the Little Stars 6" sauce, 7½" (shown), and 10" bowls are no exception. This pattern represents Millersburg's design qualities at their best, with stippled panels of stars, plain panels of flowers (that much resemble Fenton's Starflower pattern), and a border flower that is like a poinsettia.

Loganberry Vases

This beautiful vase was Imperial's #477 pattern and is found in marigold, purple, amber, green, emerald, clambroth, and smoke. The purple and the smoke are the rarest but amber seems to be prized too and the stunning iridescence on most examples explains why. This vase was part of Imperial's reproduction line in the 1960s and 1970s in marigold, green, smoke, and white but these are marked with the IG mark.

Lotus and Grape Plate

This typical Fenton pattern can be found in a bonbon, small footed bowls, a 7" to 8" medium size bowl that can be collar based or footed, a 9" larger bowl, or a large plate. Plates are found in marigold, amethyst, blue, and green but are rare in all with green being the most desired.

Lotus Land

It is believed this is one of Northwood's rarest patterns and it is hard to argue with that assumption. Found only on the two-handled bonbon or card tray shape, four or five examples are known in amethyst and a single marigold is reported. Lotus Land is seldom sold and always brings a large price when it is.

Lovely

Lovely is from Northwood, and sometimes found on the interior of their twig-footed Leaf and Beads bowls. Colors are marigold, amethyst, and green with the green being the rarest. The design is a good one, resembling some Dugan bowl patterns. Shards are reported from the Dugan factory site, but most collectors still give Northwood the credit for this one.

Many Ribs Vase

Normally found in opalescent glass from Model Flint Glass in 1902, the aqua opalescent carnival one-of-a-kind vase shown was a real surprise when it first came to light. Did Model Flint have a try at carnival in its final days? Did Northwood obtain this mould and test it? Perhaps we will never really know but the very rarity of the piece and the questions of its origin make it an important and desirable item. It stands 8" tall.

Many Stars (Millersburg)

This Millersburg pattern can be found in two variations — a large six-pointed star in the center or a rarer five-point star. The large bowls can be ice cream shape, ruffled, square, tightly crimped, or round with a three-in-one edge. In addition there is a very rare chop plate in marigold. Usual colors for the bowls are marigold, amethyst, and green, but a rare blue exists. The amethyst ice cream shaped bowl is rare and there are at least two vaseline bowls.

Mayan

Millersburg's Mayan is common in green in an ice cream shape, but here is the only reported example in marigold, and it is ruffled to boot. The design is simple but effective, consisting of six feathered fans around a large stippled center button. Sizes range from 8" to 9" depending on the shape and all items have a typical radium finish.

Mayflower Bowl

Mayflower is normally found as the exterior pattern of the Millersburg Grape Leaves bowl. It is rare enough in that capacity, but here is the only reported bowl *without* an interior pattern! It is marigold over clear (crystal examples of Mayflower are known in non-iridized glass) and it has to rank alongside the rare iridized Trefoil Finecut plate as a top Millersburg bowl rarity.

Memphis Fruit Bowl
(aqua opalescent)

This Northwood fruit bowl (the stand or base is missing) in the Memphis pattern normally wouldn't gather a great interest among collectors, but this is the only one ever reported on aqua opalescent glass. Not only is this the first fruit bowl in this color, it turns out to be the *only* piece of Memphis in any shape in this color. Sadly the bowl is cracked but it still brought a middle four-figure price when it sold on eBay.

Memphis Fruit Bowl
(ice blue)

The Memphis fruit bowl differs from the punch bowl in that the punch bowl fits *into* the round base stand while the fruit bowl is much shallower and fits *over* the octagonal base. One sees cups displayed with either (as with our fruit bowl here), but they properly belong with the punch set. Fruit bowls are found in marigold, amethyst, green, white, ice green, lime green, ice blue, and cobalt blue. All except the first three colors are rare and desirable.

Memphis Punch Set
(ice green)

The ice green Memphis punch set is a clear-cut example of Northwood's talent for making beautiful pastel carnival glass. It is extremely rare in all pastels but especially in ice green. The punch set differs from the fruit bowl in that the punch set has a round marie and fits into a round rim at the top of the base and the fruit bowl fits *over* an octagonal base.

Milady

This is one of the better designed water sets from the Fenton Company, and while not as rare as most of the patterns shown in this book it is certainly a collectors' favorite. This was their #1110 pattern, made in 1910. Records show it was made in marigold, amethyst, green, or blue. The green pieces are quite rare.

Millersburg Cherry Chop Plate

This spectacular plate is 10" in diameter and is called a chop plate. Only one example is known in each of the colors (marigold, amethyst, and the green shown), and each is rare and very desirable. Seldom do these plates come up for sale and when they do, it is at quite high prices. Some collectors call this Hanging Cherries.

Millersburg Cherry Experimental Tumbler

Only this single example of the Millersburg Cherry tumbler with enameled cherries exists, and it is a rare item indeed. It is on green glass with a strong radium finish and the cherries are a goofus red.

Millersburg Cherry Pitchers

The Millersburg Cherry milk pitcher is a rare and coveted item, much rarer than the water pitcher. They can have collar base as shown or a rare flat base like the Multi-fruits and Flowers pitcher shown elsewhere (two are known). Amethyst is a bit harder to find than the green or the marigold.

Millersburg Cherry Plate (small)

This pattern is known in the 6" plate (shown), 8" plates are known in green or amethyst, 9" plates in amethyst, and a 10" chop plate in marigold, amethyst, or green (one example of each is reported). All plates in this Millersburg pattern are very rare and sell for sizable prices when sold.

Millersburg Cherry Powder Jar

This pattern, also known as Hanging Cherries, is found in water sets, table sets, a large compote, a berry set, a 7" (medium) bowl, a small 6" plate, an 11" chop plate, a milk pitcher, a bowl with a rare hobnail exterior, and the rare powder jars with lids shown. The colors presently known in this powder jar are green, marigold, marigold-over-milk glass, and two or three non-iridized milk glass examples. Both the marigold and the marigold-over-milk glass examples were discovered in the last three years. Shards (primarily in milk glass) of this powder jar were found in the Millersburg factory site digs by John Calai so there is no doubt of the maker. The fruits and the finely veined leaves and textured stems are very realistic. All colors and treatments in this powder jar are very rare and very desirable.

Millersburg Elks

Only two shapes are known in the Millersburg Elks pieces: the 7½" bowl and the solid glass paperweight, both shown. The bowl is found only in amethyst, usually with a radium finish, and is known as the "two-eyed elk," distinguishing it from similar pieces by Fenton. It is found either ruffled or in an ice cream shape. The paperweight is almost an inch thick and is 4" long and 2⅝" wide. It can be found in green or amethyst. Both items are quite rare and very desirable.

Millersburg Flute Vase

The vase shown here is really a whimsey. While it was warm it was pulled into a vase form from a bowl shape like the one found on the Millersburg large Strawberry Wreath bowls. These vases are quite rare, very desirable, and bring big money. Colors are amethyst (two – three known), green (two confirmed), and blue (two or three reported).

Millersburg Peacock Plate

Seldom found, this 6½" plate in the Millersburg Peacock pattern has no bee near the bird's beak and was flattened from the small sauce bowl. Found mostly in amethyst, only the single marigold example shown has surfaced. Even the known amethyst examples number less than one dozen.

Millersburg Plates (Peacock, Peacock and Urn)

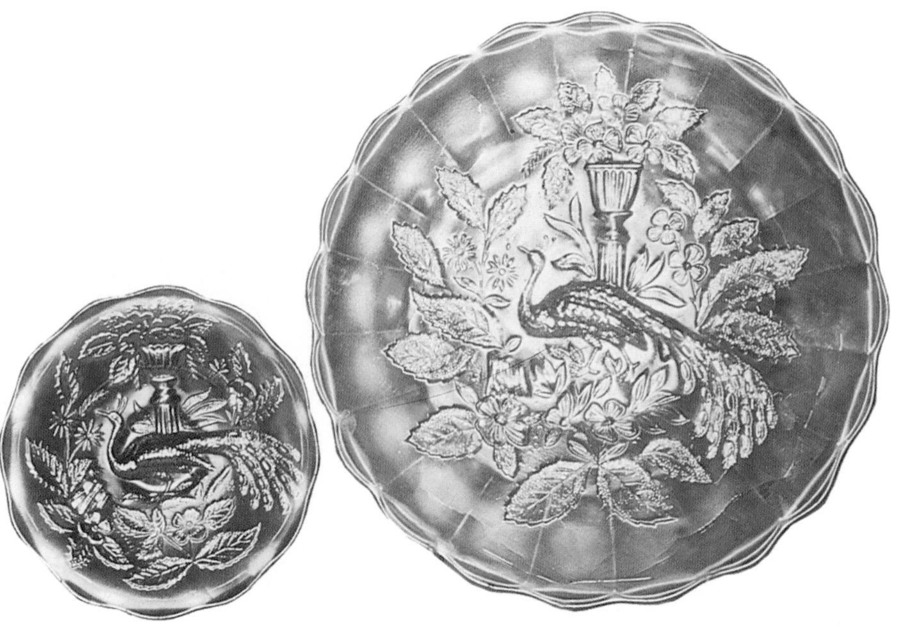

These are two different patterns from Millersburg that contain peacocks. The plate shapes are quite rare, especially the marigold chop plate. It is Millersburg's Peacock and Urn pattern and measures 11¼" across. It is also found in amethyst (three known) as well as marigold (four known). The smaller 6" plate in amethyst is Millersburg's Peacock pattern. It has a flared urn without beading and no bee. This plate is known in marigold (rather than amethyst) and was pulled from the small berry bowl.

Mirrored Lotus Plate

Mirrored Lotus was made by the Fenton Art Glass Company in bowls, rose bowls, and a rare plate shape. Most shapes are found in marigold, blue, and green, but the rose bowl is known in a rare white, and both the bowl and the plate are found in the very rare celeste blue shown. The exterior is the Berry and Leaf Circle pattern.

Mitered Ovals Vase

The beautiful rare Millersburg vase is one of the best in its field and is valued in *any* color. It is found in marigold, amethyst, and most often green. All colors are equally coveted. One green with a slightly aqua tint is known. Many of us have dreamed of a blue one but alas it has been only a dream. The Mitered Ovals vase is about 10" tall and always has a crimped and ruffled top.

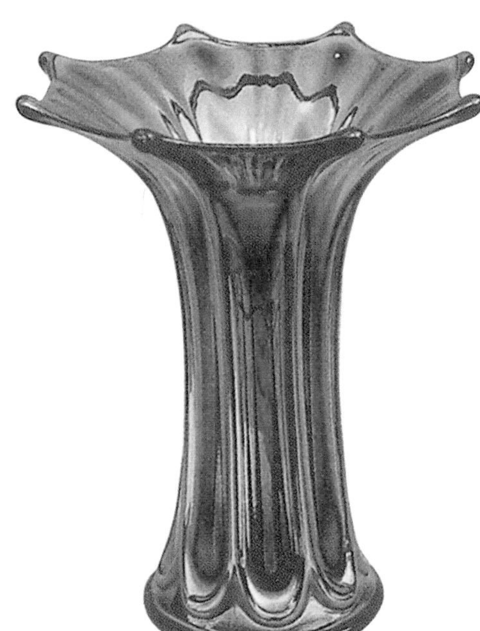

Morning Glory Vase (Imperial)

Imperial made a host of these vases in three sizes and many colors, but this very, very rare *electric* blue vase in the mid-size is in a class all its own. It has to be one of the top rarities from the Imperial Company. The stunning color and iridescence is remarkable.

Morning Glory
Water Set

This Millersburg beauty is simply regal in concept and appearance. It is one of the best water sets in carnival glass. The 11" tankard pitcher soars from a rolled base with panels and realistic morning glories, leaves, and tendrils wrapping around the center. Colors are marigold, amethyst, and the harder to find green. Less than a dozen sets in all colors are known.

Multi-Fruits and Flowers Dessert

Although sometimes called a compote, this Millersburg piece is really a short-stemmed sherbet. The first of these showed up in 1970 and caused a bit of a stir, but over the next few years, more examples came to light in both green (three known) and amethyst (five known, some with damage). These beautiful and rare items do not bring the prices many have felt they deserved.

Multi-Fruits and Flowers Pitchers

A decade ago, these water pitchers from Millersburg caused quite a stir and today they are just as rare. Five amethyst, two marigold, and one green are known. One of the amethyst examples has enameled fruit. As you can see there are two base variations in the amethyst pitchers and at least one in that color has damage. Still these are very desirable and seldom change hands.

Multi-Fruits and Flower Punch Sets

This is a beautiful Millersburg design found on punch sets, water sets, and a stemmed dessert. All pieces are rare. The punch sets are found with either flared tops (marigold, amethyst, very rare green) or tulip shaped (marigold, amethyst, green, or the very rare blue). Here are the top four sets. They include a green one with a flared top and marigold, amethyst, and blue examples with the tulip top. It is an impressive array indeed.

Nesting Swan Plate

While the purist might insist this is actually a low bowl (the edges do turn up slightly), it has been called a plate and it has a real presence that a bowl doesn't exhibit. It is green, measures 10" across, and has a strong satin finish rather than the usual Millersburg radium.

Nesting Swan Proof Bowl (green)

This bowl is a joy to behold. Besides the green one here, Marie McGee shows an amethyst example in her *Millersburg Glass* and those are the only two in this shape reported. In addition to ruffled bowls, this pattern can be found on square bowls with a candy-ribbon edge and a very rare tri-cornered bowl.

Nesting Swan Rose Bowl

This is the only Milllersburg Nesting Swan rose bowl reported. It is marigold. It is a very rare, very desirable piece of glass that would be the star in any Millersburg collection. The color is rich and dark and shows nicely against the Diamond and Fan exterior pattern.

Nesting Swan Spittoon

While it may seem hard to believe, this very rare item started out as a Nesting Swan bowl with the usual Diamond and Fan exterior and was whimsied into a spittoon shape. Since its first appearance in carnival circles, only two examples, one amethyst and one green, have been reported and most collectors would love to own one.

Night Stars

This rare Millersburg pattern can be found on olive green and marigold deep bonbons; one vaseline, one amethyst, and one green card tray; and green and amethyst spade-shaped nappies. The pattern is very distinctive with a large six-pointed star in the center and a ring of smaller stars bordered by a stylized fleur-de-lis design.

Nippon Plate

This is Northwood's version of the Peacock Tail. It is found in bowls with ruffled or pie crust edges and a 9" plate. All Nippon plates are rare, but marigold is a bit easier to find than green or amethyst. The rest of the colors (white, ice blue, or aqua opalescent) are all limited to two or three examples at most.

Norris N. Smith

This is from the Garden Mums mould like so many of Fenton's advertising items. This one says "Norris N. Smith - Real Estate and Insurance - Rome, Ga." It is found on both bowls and plates, and like the other advertising items is a collectors' favorite.

Northwood Poppy

This popular Northwood pattern is known only in the one shape. It is found in a large range of colors including marigold, green, amethyst, cobalt blue, ice blue, white, aqua, lavender, black amethyst, amber, aqua opalescent, and the very rare marigold-on-custard shown.

Northwood's Strawberry

Northwood must have liked this pattern because there are so very many colors found on the bowls, plates, and handgrip plates. Pieces may be plain or stippled on the background. The stippled pieces are more desirable. Here we show a ruffled stippled bowl in a very rare color called lime green. The glass has an almost vaseline look but with a green tint that almost lights up a room.

Nu-Art Chrysanthemum Plate

Like the Nu-Art Homestead plate shown below, this Imperial plate has been reproduced, but remains a top item for collectors. It is found in marigold, amber, clambroth, green, purple, white, and smoky blue. The design of floral sprays and fronds covers most of the space. It has a Greek Key border. Plates may be marked "Nu-Art" or not.

Nu-Art Homestead Plate

While it has been reproduced over the years this 10½" plate shape from Imperial remains a collectors' favorite. It is found in marigold, amber, purple, blue, green, white, emerald, and the smoke shown. The design features a nature scene with a Greek Key border. Plates can be signed "Nu-Art" or not.

Ogden Furniture

Like most of the advertising pieces from Fenton, this one is amethyst and can be found in ruffled bowls, ice cream shaped bowls, or plates. The lettering says "Ogden Furniture and Carpet Co. - Ogden, Utah." Pieces in this pattern are a bit on the rare side and in demand.

Ohio Star Clover-Leaf Bowl

Sometimes found in crystal, this 5½" bowl is called a clover-leaf or tri-cornered bowl and was shaped from the small sauce or ice cream bowl. In carnival glass only this single example is known and it is fabulous, with a soft marigold radium finish.

Ohio Star Green Opalescent Vase

This green opalescent Millersburg rarity on slag type glass is a spectacular find. Two of these vases have been found. One that is slightly taller and is damaged and one that is perfect (shown). For many years a collector kept these vases in a bank vault for they are just that valuable and only after her passing did they come up for auction. Both extremely rare and desirable, this fine vase is a collector's dream and deserves its lofty standing in carnival glass vases.

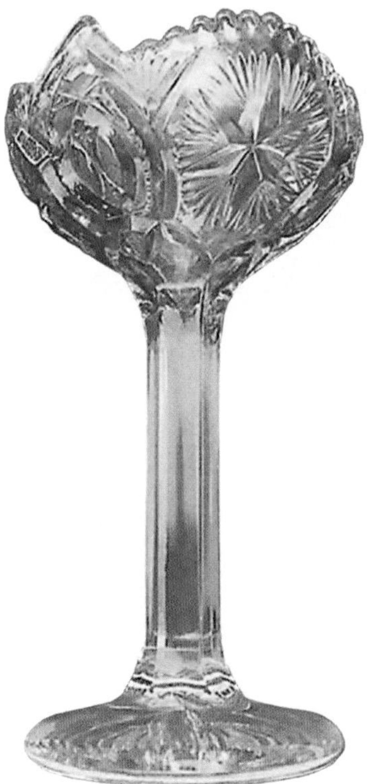

Ohio Star Tall Compote

Found in both crystal and marigold carnival glass, this tall compote from the Millersburg Company is a gem. The stem is solid glass and *may* be clear (but not on the one shown). It is found in two shapes: deeply cupped or shallow and ruffled. Only a few are known in either shape and all are very desirable.

Ohio Star Vases

While not quite in the class of the rare green opalescent vase we show on page 132, the regular colors in this fine shape are jewels in their own right and bring high prices when they are occasionally sold. Colors are marigold, amethyst, green, clambroth, and two examples in white carnival. Amethyst is the easiest to find (relatively speaking), with green next, and then marigold. Clambroth is rarest of those four but doesn't bring the price of green or amethyst.

Ohio Star Vase Whimsey

The Millersburg Ohio Star pattern is well known with carnival or crystal glass collectors and while the standard vases are not rare, this pulled or stretched version is. The example shown has been pulled from a 10" size to a remarkable 17½" tall and still retains its design quite well. Most collectors who have seen these whimsies have nothing but respect for them and few ever trade hands once they are purchased. At least three green and two or three amethyst examples exist but surely marigold was made and just hasn't been reported yet.

Olympic Compote

This Millersburg rarity uses the same exterior mould as the Leaf and Little Flowers compote. It is 3" tall and about 3" in diameter. The exterior has a wide panel or flute pattern and an octagonal base. Only two of these rare compotes are reported: one in green and one in amethyst shown here. The interior design consists of a star center within a circle of beading and a garland with flowers around the bowl.

Orange Tree (Stylized Flower Center)

Orange Tree is one of Fenton's most prolific patterns. The plate shapes have come into their own and are collectors' favorites. Currently collectors call the center variation a "trunk center" but it was named Stylized Flower in the 1970s by Marion Hartung. It simply means the bark on the trunk seems to extend down into the center of the piece and can be found on some bowls and plates. Orange Tree plates (9" diameter) are rare, desirable, and pricey in amethyst, green, aqua opalescent, ice green, and blue.

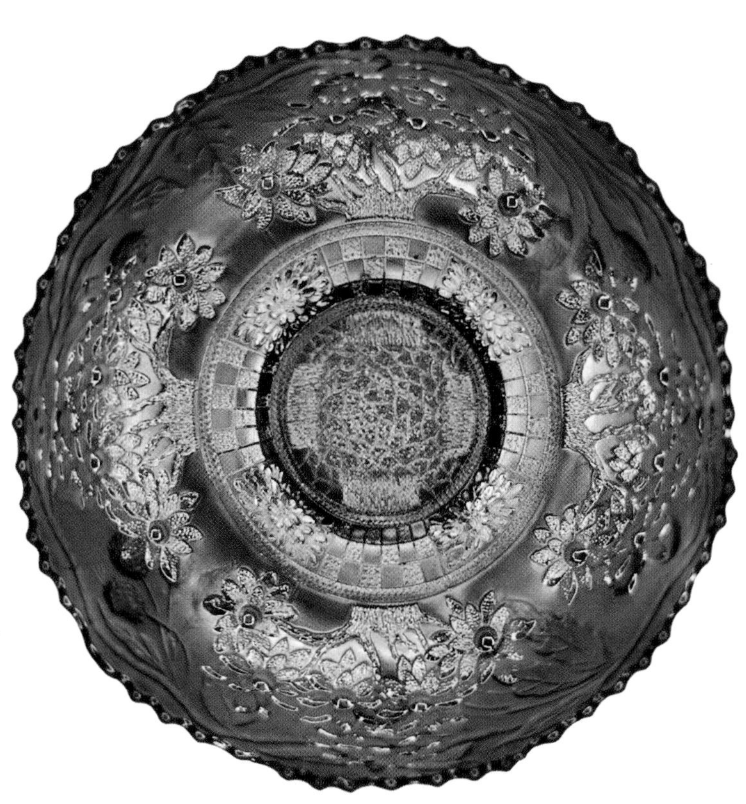

Orange Tree Bowl (red)

While red is a bit of a common color in this large Orange Tree bowl, it still brings a hefty price at auction. This is one red item collectors seem to like despite its lack of real rarity. The orange tree's design shows well and as you can see, it doesn't have the Stylized Flower center.

Orange Tree Centerpiece Bowl

This Fenton rarity, whimsied from the large footed bowl, is a massive beauty. One amethyst example is known and here is the first reported green one. The upper edges have been rolled out evenly with no ruffling, giving the bowl a shallow look that is most pleasing and desirable.

Orange Tree Loving Cup

This very pretty and well designed handled loving cup is part of Fenton's Orange Tree pattern. It can be found in marigold, amethyst, green, blue, peach opalescent (one), white, ice blue (one), and the aqua opalescent shown (one). It stands nearly 6" tall and has Fenton's Peacock Tail pattern on the interior.

Orange Tree Orchard Urn Whimsey

The Orange Tree Orchard from the Fenton Art Glass Company was a companion pattern to their regular Orange Tree line. It is usually found in water sets. Here we have the only known urn, whimsied from the water pitcher. To achieve this, a second handle was added and the lip was rolled into a vase top. The color is a strong marigold with a fine satin finish and the overall look is sensational.

Orange Tree Spittoon Whimsey

Carnival glass patterns that are whimsied into spittoon or cuspidor shapes nearly always draw great attention, and this rare example, pulled from the base of a powder jar in the Orange Tree pattern, is no different. It is marigold and the first piece reported in this pattern and shape so it is very desirable.

Oriental Poppy Pitcher

Oriental Poppy is one of Northwood's well-known patterns. It was produced in crystal, sapphire blue, or emerald green (the latter two often with gilding). It was then produced in water sets as part of their carnival glass line. Colors are marigold, green, amethyst, blue, white, ice blue, ice green, and this rare powder blue color. It stands a shade darker than ice blue and ranks with ice green as a top color for this pitcher.

Oriental Poppy Variant

The Oriental Poppy design is a well-known Northwood pattern and rates very high in water sets in the rarer colors of ice green, ice blue, and cobalt blue. Other colors such as marigold or amethyst seem a bit plentiful but the marigold example we show is a different matter. It has interior ribbing that runs from the base to near the top. There are 24 ribs and this is the first piece with this interior reported. There is also a rare 11" ruffled bowl.

Paneled Dandelion Lamp

The blue shade for this extreme rarity from Fenton once rested with two taller green candlesticks but it is finally with the correct candle base and is now a one-of-a-kind beauty. The pattern is Fenton's Paneled Dandelions and for a pattern that was used only for water sets, a great number of rarities and whimsies seem to exist.

Paneled Dandelion Vase Whimsey

The Fenton Art Glass Company produced the Paneled Dandelion tankard water set starting in 1910 in carnival glass. It is a stately, well-designed pattern and well-liked by collectors. But the real excitement of this pattern comes with its two rarities: a very rare candle-lamp and the vase whimsey shown here. It is cobalt blue and from the pitcher mould where the handle has been left off (you can see the oval where it would have been joined) and the top has been ruffled.

Paneled Holly Pitcher

For many years this one iridized water pitcher in Paneled Holly has been the only known example. It is amethyst with a great satin finish and has been in the same collection for about 25 years. Its rarity and desirability go without saying.

Paneled Tree Trunk Vase

Some collectors call this a jardiniere shape (flared from a vase). It was made by the Dugan Glass Company around 1910 and is known in marigold, amethyst, green, and peach opalescent. All colors are rare. These vases range in size from 6" tall to roughly 9" tall, and usually have a very flared top with the panels ending in spikes pulled into flames.

Panther (Nile green opalescent)

Only this single example of this master bowl in the Panther pattern from Fenton has ever been reported. It is on Nile green opaque glass that has been iridized and has an opalescent treatment. Someone at the factory must have really wanted to give this piece every treatment imaginable.

Panther Centerpiece Bowl

While this bowl is also known in marigold, it is this blue bowl with fantastic iridescence that is the show-stopper. It is the large 10" bowl that has been pulled out to a shallow shape and then the lip is softly rolled upward, giving it an ice cream shape.

Peacock and Urn (blue)

Normally found in marigold, amethyst, and green, this large (9½" – 10") ice cream bowl is extremely rare in vaseline and the blue shown. Please note that the urn has no beading. The coloring is a very vivid blue, a very unusual shade for Millersburg, and the iridescence is striking and electric. This is about as good as it gets, friends.

Peacock and Urn Giant Compote

Part of Millersburg's Peacock and Urn pattern, this very rare and desirable compote is 7¼" tall and 8½" wide. It is found in amethyst, green, marigold, and the very rare clambroth (one known). Its exterior is the clover-based wide panel design that was first a Crystal Glass Company mould and then came to Millersburg in 1909.

Peacock at the Fountain Compote

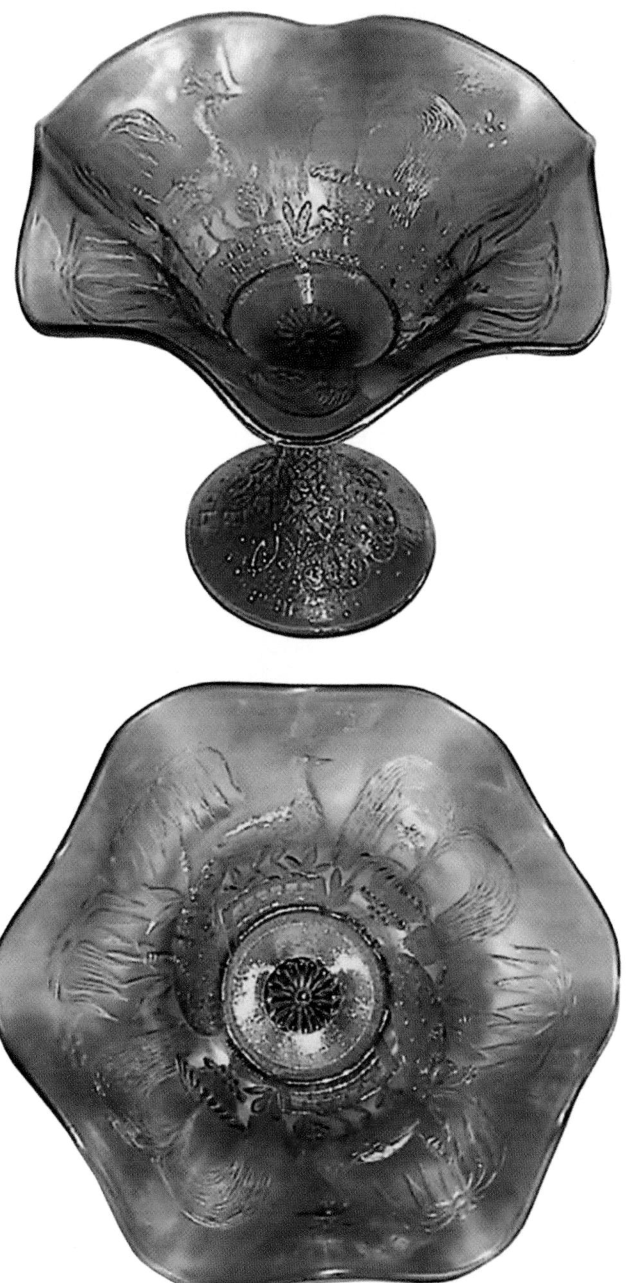

This beautiful Northwood compote with Peacock at the Fountain on the interior and Hearts and Flowers on the exterior is a real find. Colors are all scarce with white, amethyst, marigold, blue, ice blue, and ice green a bit easier to find than the aqua opalescent. But here is the first reported compote in green and it is a real beauty, tops for both rarity and desirability.

Peacock at the Fountain Cup Whimsey

This Northwood whimsey that was pulled from a punch cup into a vessel with a spout is a very desirable item. It is the only example reported at this time and therefore is a real rarity. The color is amethyst with very strong satin iridescence that shows gold, bronze, and blue highlights.

Peacock at the Fountain Orange Bowl

This massive footed fruit bowl or orange bowl from Northwood is a very desirable item. It is known in marigold, amethyst, green, cobalt blue, white, ice green, horehound, and the aqua opalescent shown. Aqua opalescent and green are the rarest colors followed by white, ice green, and horehound.

Peacock at the Fountain Orange Bowl Whimsey

Although usually found in a ruffled shape, this footed fruit bowl has been shaped with the points straight up (just as it came from the mould). Some collectors call this a deep centerpiece bowl. It is found in marigold and the amethyst shown but is very rare. The color is almost electric.

Peacock at the Fountain Punch Set (aqua opalescent)

This Northwood Peacock at the Fountain punch set is one of four known in this wonderful aqua opalescent color (some spare cups and bases are also known). At this time the auction price for such a set would be in the high five figures but seldom does one of these beauties go on the market.

Peacock at the Fountain Spittoon

This very rare Northwood whimsey, fashioned from the base of the table set's covered sugar, is one of the company's top draws in this field. One amethyst and one green example currently are known and the prices each has brought are staggering. Peacock at the Fountain was first produced in 1912 and was patented in 1914. (Diamond copied the water set and a patent, though unusual, was probably warranted in this case.)

Peacock Banana Bowl (Millersburg)

Just as the spittoon whimsies and the rose bowl whimsies in this pattern are very high on the desirability list, so is this a banana bowl whimsey. Two examples are known at this time: one amethyst and the other the vaseline shown.

Peacock Garden Vase

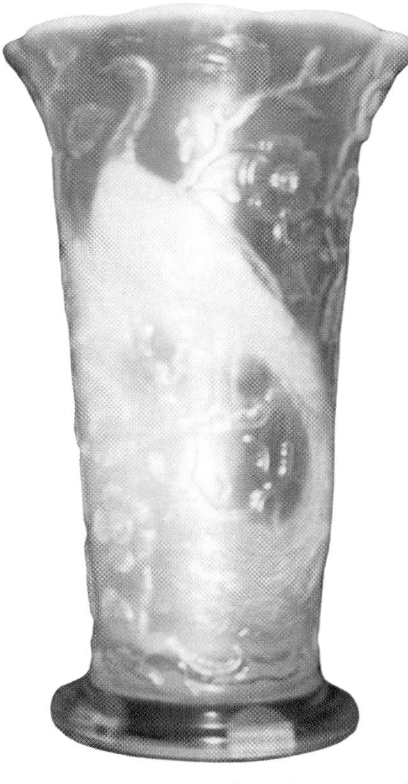

In carnival glass this rare and very desirable vase is known in four marigold, two white, one white opalescent, and two Cameo vases. (The Cameo vases are probably Fenton pieces.) It is believed Northwood first made this vase and then Fenton continued production in 1933 as their #791 vase. Fenton made them in many colors and treatments that are collectible in their own right. Iridized Peacock Garden vases seldom come up for sale.

Peacock Mould-Proof Bowl (Millersburg)

This bowl is just as it came from the mould with no additional shaping and is called a mould-proof bowl by collectors. It measures about 8" across and nearly 5" deep, has a fine radium finish, and while it doesn't bring a high price at this time, is a very collectible rarity.

Peacock Rose Bowl (Millersburg)

This rose bowl shape was pulled from a large bowl into a whimsey that is fantastic. One marigold, one amethyst, and the one vaseline shown have been reported. Surely a green example was made but none has ever been reported. These three single examples are some of the best rose bowl pieces carnival glass.

Peacocks (On the Fence)

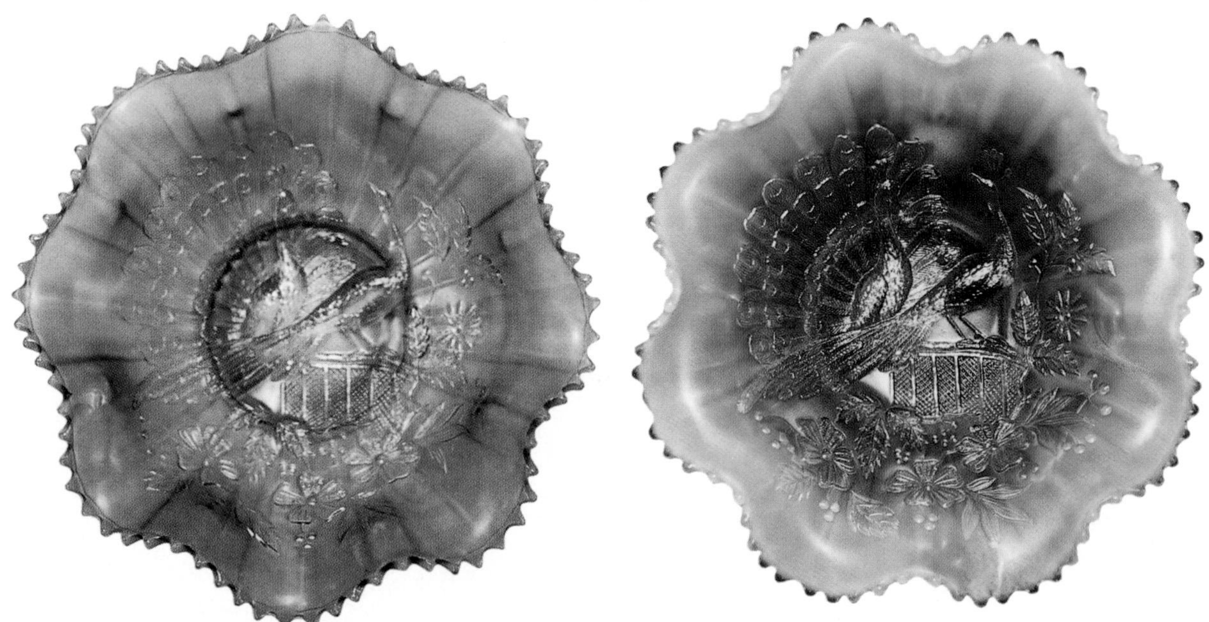

This pattern is a beauty in either bowls or plates. The color range is wide, especially in bowls, and includes vivids and pastels. Pieces may be found with or without a stippled center and edges may be ruffled or pie crust. Here is a very rare smoke bowl and a favorite aqua opalescent bowl. Other rare colors include honey amber, horehound, ice green, ice blue, lavender, ice blue opalescent, pearlized custard, lime green opalescent, and powder blue opalescent.

Peacock Spittoon (Millersburg)

There are two very rare spittoon whimsies shaped from the large bowl known in this famous Millersburg pattern. One is marigold and one is amethyst. Either would be a Millersburg collector's dream and both are equally rare. And this is one spittoon whimsey where the interior design is easy to see!

Peacock Square Bowl (Millersburg)

While we've seen this same bowl in a tri-cornered shape, this appears to be the first square one. (Square bowls are known in the small size in amethyst or marigold.) It is a great green with the radium blue finish for which Millersburg was so famous. The luster just seems to grab you and that was what Millersburg carnival glass was all about.

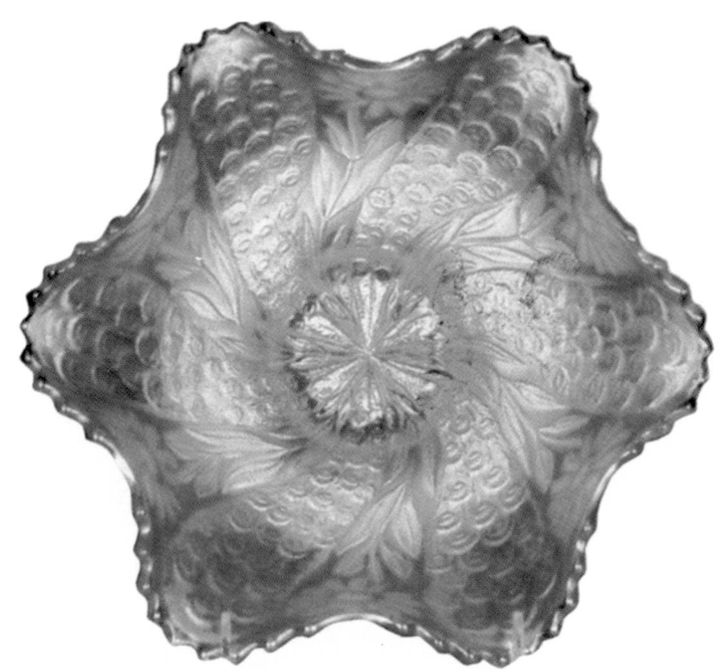

Peacock Tail and Daisy

Now believed to be a Westmoreland pattern, this rare bowl has a real presence and is very desirable. It is found in marigold, amethyst, and blue iridized milk glass. The design is a good one with a pinwheel of peacock tails that twist from the center to the outer edge.

Peacock Tail Chop Plate

This well known Fenton pattern is familiar to most collectors. It is found in many shapes including small 7" plates, medium 9" plates, and this single 11" chop plate. It was produced in 1911 and is sometimes called Flowering Almonds by collectors. The pattern has never shown better than on this rare plate.

Peacock Tail Spittoon

This Fenton creation is normally an easy pattern to find. It is mostly found in bowls, compotes, a bonbon, hats, and plates. Here is the only reported example of a spittoon whimsey. It is in cobalt blue and was shaped from a bowl. It stands 3" tall.

Penny and Gentles Plate

At the time of this writing, only this one double-handgrip plate has been reported. It is lettered "Penny and Gentles - Broadway and Morgan." It is high on the list of lettered or advertised rarities and created a stir when it first came to light.

People's Vase

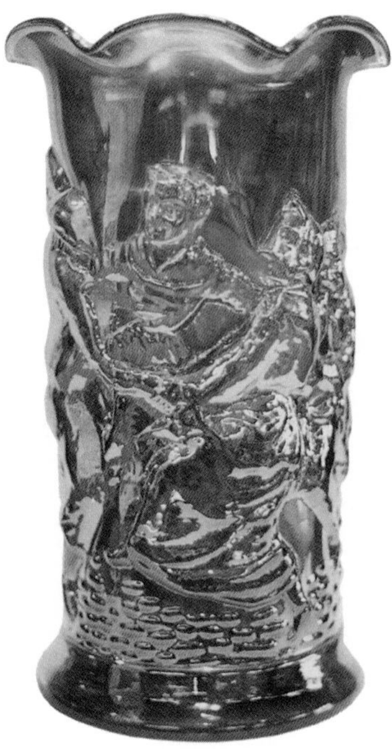

This Millersburg masterpiece is the absolute king of all carnival glass vases. It was their #70, called a Holland vase. These are hefty items, weighing five pounds and standing 11" tall. They are rare in any color. Only one marigold, five amethyst, one green, and one blue are known. All the amethyst vases (except one) have ruffled tops, while the marigold, blue, and green vases have straight tops. The design is of children dancing on a cobbled street while an old man watches them.

Perfection

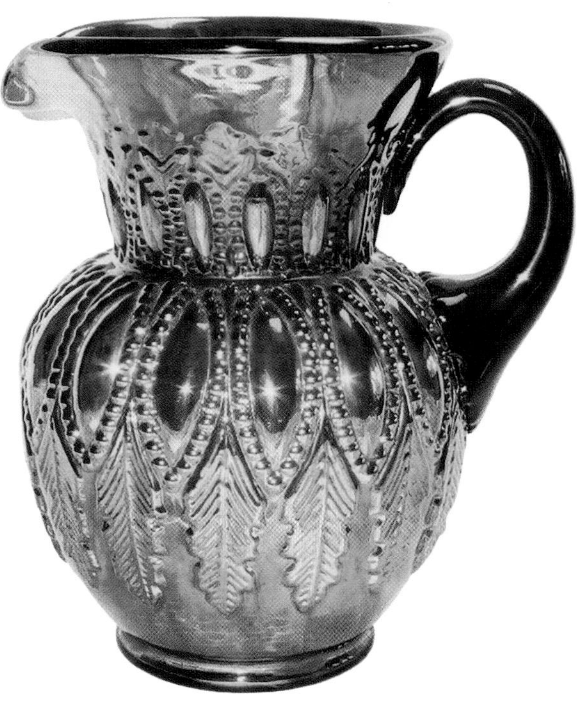

Perfection is one of Millerburg's better water sets. It is a beautifully designed pattern similar to the Gay 90s except for the vastly different shapes. The tops of the pitchers can be flared (as shown) or ruffled. Colors are marigold, amethyst, or green. The pitcher stands about 9" tall. Tumblers are quite rare in marigold. The design contains a row of acanthus leaves with beaded ovals separating them, giving a simple but effective overall pattern. All colors are rare and bring hefty prices when sold.

Persian Garden Chop Plate

Found in three colors, amethyst, white, and peach opalescent, this massive 11" – 12" chop plate is a collectors' dream. It was produced by the Dugan Glass Company and continued by the Diamond Company. The exterior carries the Big Basketweave pattern and when held to the light, the two patterns seem to mingle and intertwine magically.

Persian Garden Punch Bowl

Some collectors call this a round fruit bowl but the depth gives it more of a punch bowl look. Here is one of the two marigold examples known. It is also found on a single amethyst example. The exterior is the Big Basketweave pattern on the base and a trellis-like variation on the bowl. Persian Garden was first a Dugan pattern and carried over to the Diamond Company's later production. This piece is a very underpriced rarity.

Persian Medallion Centerpiece Bowl

Even in the large ruffled fruit bowl from this mould, green is rare and desirable. To find it in the only reported centerpiece with the points turned in evenly like a rose bowl is extraordinary. The exterior pattern is Fenton's Grape and Cable which gives a massive look to the pattern.

Persian Medallion Footed Bowl

It was a real surprise in 2000 when the two examples of this large Persian Medallion bowl first surfaced. The interior mould has been merged with the footed exterior mould of the Water Lily bowl with a 4½" flat marie! Both known bowls are cobalt blue and have a three-in-one ruffling on the edges.

Persian Medallion Spittoon

This very rare and desirable item was whimsied from the small bowl mould. It is green and the only one reported. The iridescence is outstanding with a typical Fenton finish of gold and bronze highlights. Spittoon whimsies are one of the most desirable shapes in all of carnival glass and this one is right up there with the best.

Petals

Petals never really caused much excitement in the usual colors of marigold, amethyst, and green. But the appearance of this rare cobalt blue compote and then a rare ice blue example raised the rating of this Northwood pattern a bit. At the present time a couple of these are known in ice blue and there may be a second cobalt blue.

Peter Rabbit

Petter Rabbit is a companion to Fenton's Coral and Little Fishes patterns. It can be found on scarce 8½" bowls or rare 9½" plates. Colors are marigold, green, and blue for the bowls and marigold, green, blue, and a rare amber for plates. The design has a border of rabbits between trees with an "x-wreath" above and below. This is the same wreath found on Coral and Little Fishes, indicating one designer did all three patterns.

Pipe Humidor

This very rare and desirable humidor is beautifully designed and molded. It is about 8" tall and 5" across. It has a three-pronged sponge holder inside the lid and the top is a flawless pipe in high relief (a mould maker's nightmare). The base has a wreath of acorns and tobacco leaves. About a half dozen amethyst, marigold, and green examples known.

Plaid

There is something about this pattern that is fascinating. It is found on large bowls or plates. Colors on bowls include marigold, amethyst, cobalt blue, green, red (desirable), and celeste blue (very rare). On plates only marigold, amethyst, blue, or red are known. One can only imagine what a stir a green or celeste blue plate would make.

Plums and Cherries

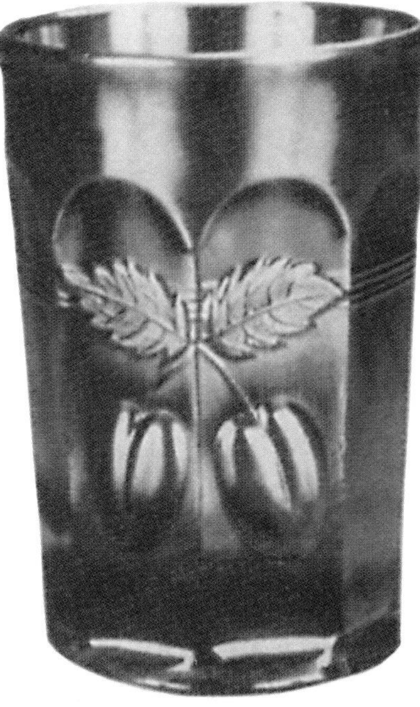

Called Two Fruits by one of the early carnival writers, this pattern is now known as Plums and Cherries. Only three pieces are reported in iridized glass. These include a tumbler in cobalt blue, a spooner in cobalt blue, and a covered sugar with the lid missing in amethyst. All three pieces are marked Northwood and all are rare and treasured.

Poinsettia Lattice (ice blue)

Poinsettia Lattice is, without question, one of Northwood's most beautiful patterns and always desired by collectors. It is found only on 8" – 9" footed bowls. Colors include marigold, amethyst, green, cobalt blue, white, ice blue (shown), aqua opalescent, and horehound. Green is the rarest of the vivid colors and white, ice blue, and aqua opalescent the rarest of pastels.

Pony (aqua)

Pony was made by Diamond Glass in around 1920 or 1921. It is easy to find in marigold and harder to find in amethyst. Occasionally ice green examples turn up but the aqua with marigold iridescence shown is much rarer. Only two bowls have been reported. Pony can be found on the plate shape too but not in the rare colors. Both bowls and plates were reproduced by L.G. Wright in the 1980s.

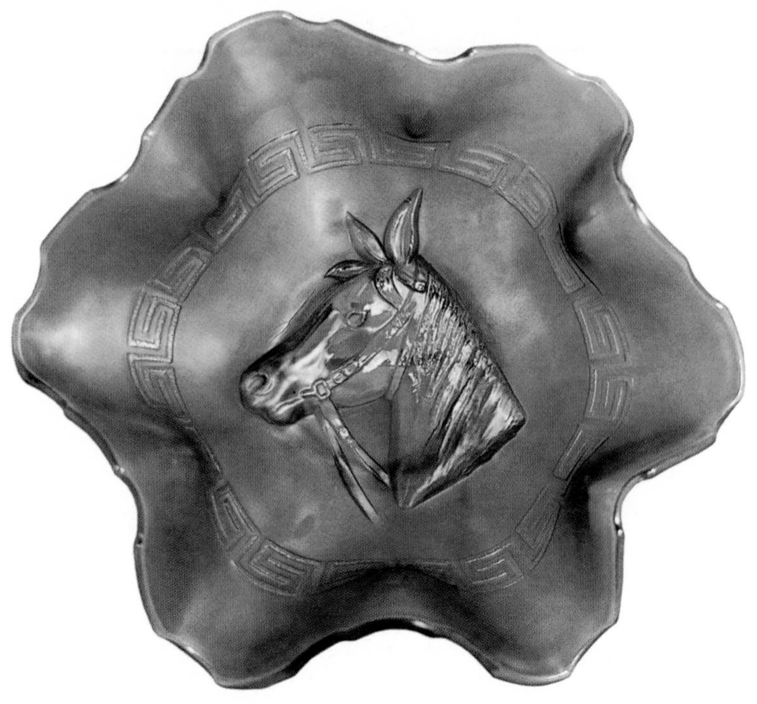

Poppy Salver (Millersburg)

This Millerburg jewel is found on large compotes and shallow salvers. It has Potpourri on the exterior. It stands about 7" tall and measures nearly 9" across the rim. The compote shape isn't rare, but the salver is, with only one marigold, one amethyst, and two green known.

Poppy Show

This beautiful pattern is a carnival collectors' favorite, credited to the Northwood Company from moulds from George Mortimer, owner of Mortimer Glass (a supply company, not a producer). It is found in many colors. The rarest color is aqua opalescent, known in two bowls (shown) and one plate. One look at either will tell you why. The design is heavy and stands out from the background in high relief.

Poppy Show Lamp Base Whimsey

This is one of two examples reported of this Imperial lamp base made from their well known vase mould. The other is actually on the original lamp. Both examples are marigold and create a real show with their size and design.

Poppy Show Plate

While not as rare as aqua opalescent or even ice green, this electric blue plate is however a stunner that grabs you. The design is one of Northwood's best and most collectors want to own either a bowl or the rarer plate. Colors are white, marigold, blue, green, ice green, amethyst, ice blue, and aqua opalescent. White is the easiest to find.

Poppy Show Vase

Poppy Show was listed in old Imperial catalogs as #488. It can be found only in the mammoth 12" vases, a table lamp, and a purple hurricane lamp. Colors of the vases are marigold, pastel marigold, amber, smoke, clambroth, green, and purple. Smoke and purple are the most desired colors. This pattern was reproduced in the 1960s, 1970s, and perhaps since, mostly in colors not made originally.

Potpourri Milk Pitcher

Potpourri is normally an exterior pattern on Millersburg's Poppy compotes in marigold, amethyst, or green. But here it is on the very desirable milk pitcher. Only about three examples have been reported in marigold and one in amethyst. The Potpourri pattern is a variation of Millersburg's Country Kitchen pattern.

Prayer Rug

Prayer Rug was made by the Fenton Company as one of their custard patterns (1912 – 1915) and advertised as Peach Blo. Iridized pieces are quite scarce. They consist of a bonbon, a rare 7½" plate, and one creamer. Prices for the plate have soared in the last few years, and the price of the creamer would certainly do the same if and when it came up for sale.

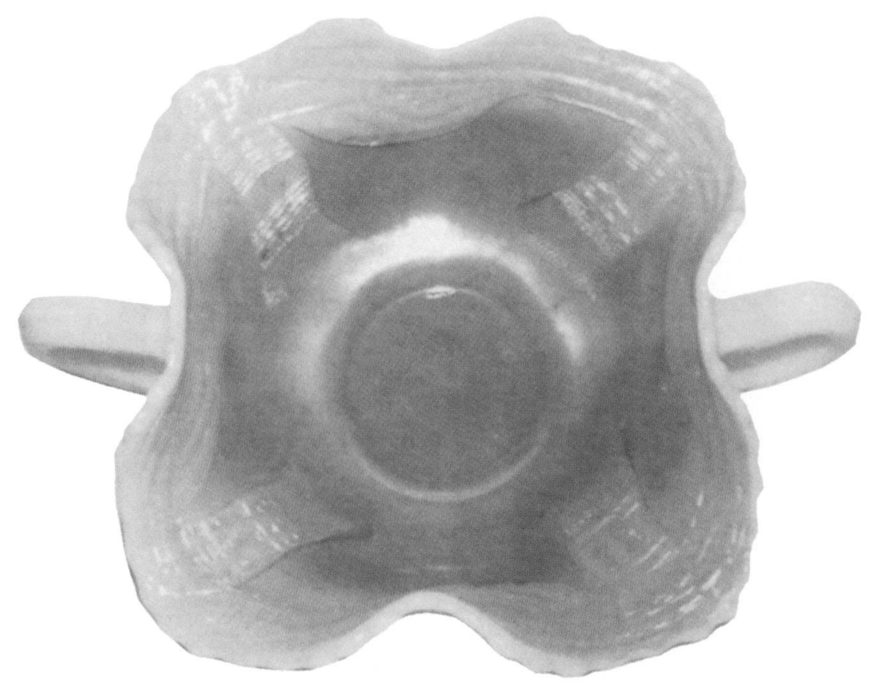

Primrose (blue)

This Millersburg pattern is not considered very desirable *except* for the three known blue bowls. One is an ice cream shape, one has six ruffles, and the one shown has a beautiful three-in-one edge. Please notice the very unusual pink iridescence. It is the only piece of Millersburg reported in this treatment.

Primrose Experimental Bowl

This strange bowl had a gilded finish applied over the Fine Cut Heart exterior and the Primrose interior before iridization. All of the flowers and leaves have a heavy gold finish. In addition, the finish isn't the typical Millersburg radium but a heavy blue and gold satin luster. We know of two Primrose bowl and one Peacock and Urn bowl with gilding.

Princess Lamp

Here is the *complete* lamp with its original shade that matches the design on the lamp's base. It was reportedly made by U.S. Glass and is often found with a shade with the Lined Lattice pattern from Dugan. Highly desirable, these lamps are treasured by collectors. The coloring is a dark amethyst with iridescence on the exterior only.

Pulled Husk Corn Vase

There are actually two versions of this strange rarity by the Northwood Company: the vase with the husks pulled and curled out and a vase that has the husks carried in higher relief. Only one of the latter is known and that is amethyst and of the former both amethyst and green examples exist. Each one is trademarked. Just why Northwood deviated from their standard Corn Vase is a mystery but here it is.

Queen's Lamp

This rare and beautiful lamp is somewhat of a mystery. It was once believed to be from Millersburg, but no longer. It is found in crystal with a matching shade and in a green iridized version (at least four are verified). The lamp is 9" tall with a 7" diameter base. They are very desirable and rarely change owners.

Quill Water Set

This rare and much sought water set is beautifully designed. It was made in non-carnival in 1907 and then in 1909 in carnival. The tumblers are pressed but the pitchers are mould-blown with applied handles. The only colors known are rare marigold or rarer amethyst. Either is eagerly purchased when offered for sale.

Raspberry Water Pitcher

This Northwood water pitcher is easily found in marigold and amethyst, harder to locate in green, a bit rare in ice blue and white, and very rare in cobalt blue and ice green. Besides the water sets, Raspberry is also known in a milk pitcher in all the same colors except blue, and there is a footed occasional piece that is readily found in marigold, amethyst, and green, and a scarce teal.

Rays and Ribbons Banana Bowl

This banana bowl whimsey from Millersburg is a rare, one-of-a-kind beauty. Only the single green and a single amethyst have been reported. Either would grace the very best of collections, especially those of Millersburg glass.

Ribbed Tornado Vase

Just why there are so many variations of the Northwood Tornado vase is a bit of a mystery, but here is one that is ribbed. It is about 6½" tall and can be found in marigold, amethyst, white, cobalt blue, and the rare ice blue shown. Actually all ribbed vases are rare so that just makes the ice blue that much more so.

Rood's Chocolates

Here is one of the four examples of this rare plate and it is about as plain as an advertising piece can get. Only the lettering: "Rood's Chocolates – Pueblo" runs through the center of the plate (much like the Broecker's Flour and the Ballard pieces). Nonetheless, it is quite desirable and brings a sizable price when sold.

Rosalind
Short Stemmed Compote

This shorter stemmed compote is 6" tall and has a round base rather than the octagon one on taller compotes. It is found in amethyst or green. It isn't as stately as its taller counterpart but is still very rare and desirable. These are rarely traded and seldom discussed.

Rosalind Tall Jelly Compote

This wonderful pattern from Millersburg is found in three sizes of bowls, a 9" plate, a short 6" compote, and the 9" jelly compote. The pattern is also found on the interior of Millersburg Dolphin compotes. A single blue example of that is shown elsewhere in this book. All the compotes are scarce to rare. The cobalt blue shown here is the rarest. It has to be rated one of the top compotes in all of carnival glass and is about as beautiful as compotes can be.

Rose Columns Experimental Vase

Besides the rare colors of marigold, amethyst, green, and blue, this very desirable vase from the Millersburg Glass Company is known in the rare amethyst decorated example shown here. The flowers have been decorated in gold and red before the iridescence was added giving the piece an exceptional beauty. Rose Columns vases are mould blown with the columns of flowers standing out in a puffy relief. They stand about 9½" tall and have a base diameter of 4½". At least two blue examples are reported and these are very costly. Green vases are the most plentiful with amethyst a very close second and marigold a distant third. The experimental example shown here is the only reported example in this treatment.

Rose Pinwheel

This 9" mystery bowl is found in marigold, green, and the lone amethyst shown. The design is much like Imperial's Acanthus but has five roses at the edges and a puffed look like the Roses and Greek Key plates shown elsewhere. The maker is unknown at this time.

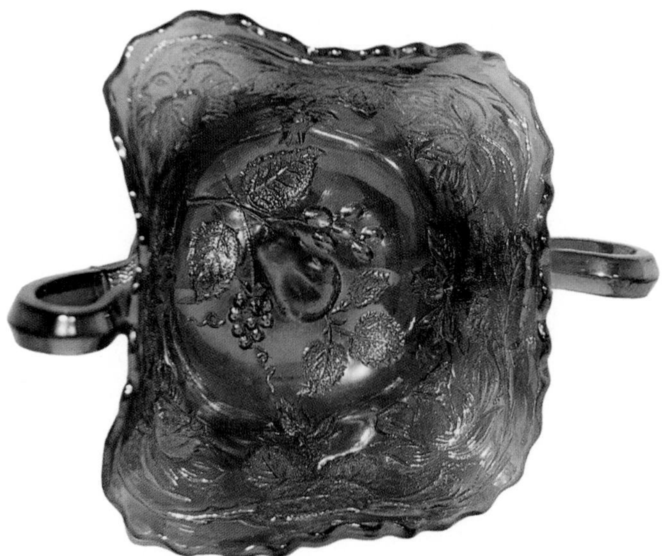

Roses and Fruit Bonbon

Roses and Fruit, from Millersburg, is found in only the stemmed bonbon. This rather rare pattern is found in marigold, amethyst, green, and ultra-rare blue (two known). The design is one rose on each corner with a pear, gooseberries, other berries, and leaves in a very natural presentation.

Roses and Greek Key

This unusual square plate is about 10" across (from point to point diagonally) with a border of puffed roses and center bands of Greek Key and bands of flowers. Only two or three of these are known: one in marigold and the amber with the distinctive smoky hue. The maker is unknown at this time.

Roses and Ruffles Lamp

This beautiful 22" GWTW lamp has become a collectors' favorite. The fittings are solid brass and the glass globes are well designed. Colors are mostly a honey-marigold but the very rare red exists and brings very real money.

Rose Show Plate (ice green)

This ice green Rose Show plate is a real beauty. While it is not as rare as the lime green plate shown below, it is a collectors' favorite and always has a strong following at auction. The coloring is a rich light green with a strong satin finish.

Rose Show Plate (lime green)

Like the Poppy Show pattern, the Rose Show pattern is one of Northwood's best and is very popular with collectors. Bowls and plates come in a host of colors. Here is the very rare lime green opalescent plate and it is a beauty! The green has just a touch of yellow and the opalescence gives a highlight to every high spot on the piece.

Rose Show Variant

Just why Northwood came up with two variations of the Rose Show pattern is a question without an answer, but here is the variant with its sawtoothed edge and a ribbed background. Plate colors are limited to marigold, cobalt blue, Renninger blue, and the very rare amethyst shown.

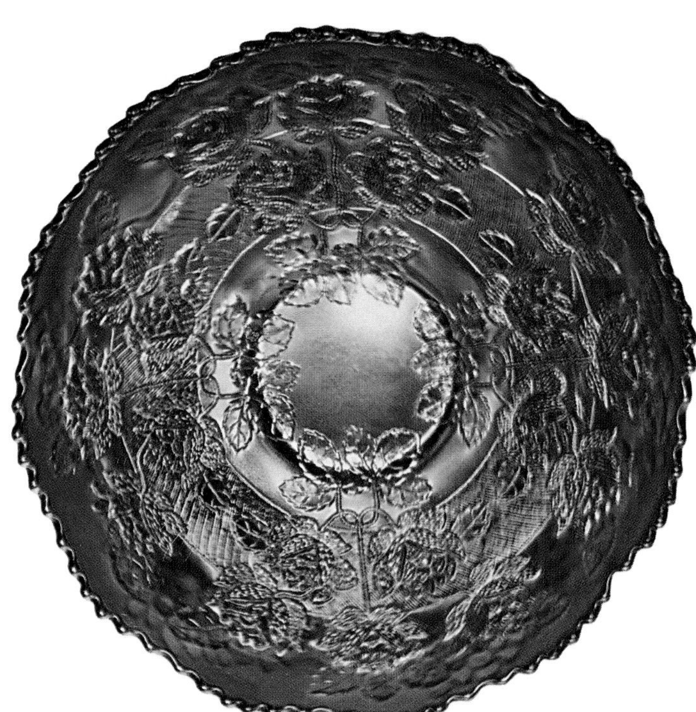

Rose Tree

Rose Tree is found on a 10" collar base bowl with Orange Tree as an exterior pattern. This Fenton design has strength in the large roses and ribbed banding that fill the space. The size is very appealing to collectors. Colors are cobalt blue and marigold. Both are rare and desirable.

Rustic Pinched Jardiniere

With as many Rustic vases that were made by the Fenton Art Glass Company (their #517), it seems very odd indeed that so few whimsey shapes exist. Here is one of the better ones. The vase is nearly like it came out of the mould, slightly pinched in at the middle and then flared a bit at the top. It is cobalt blue carnival and is, to the best of our knowledge, the only reported example in this size and shape.

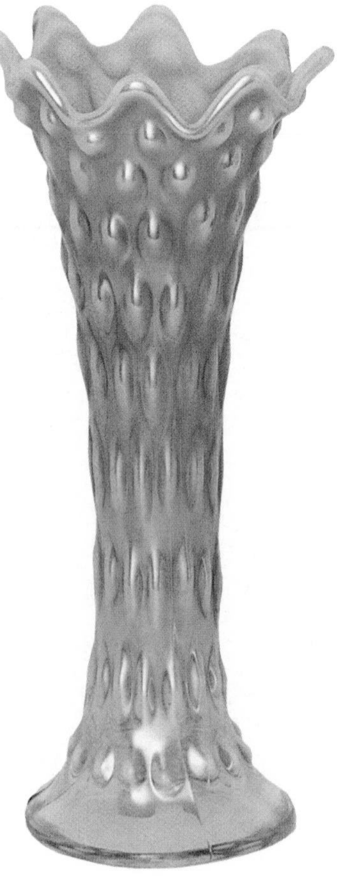

Rustic Variant Vase

While usually lumped in with Fenton's well known #517 Rustic vase, this variant was their #507. It has nine rows of hobs; #517 has eleven. The vase shown has a 3" base diameter and is a very rare peach opalescent color (one of two reported). This vase is also known in a lime green opalescent treatment that is equally as rare.

Scroll and Flower Panels

This seldom discussed, rare pattern from Imperial Glass is found in marigold, purple, and smoke (we show a rare smoke in our encyclopedia). The vase is 10" tall and was Imperial's #480 pattern. There are about five purple and two smoke reported and the rest out there are marigold. This vase was reproduced in the 1960s in marigold and smoke but are IG marked.

Scroll and Grape

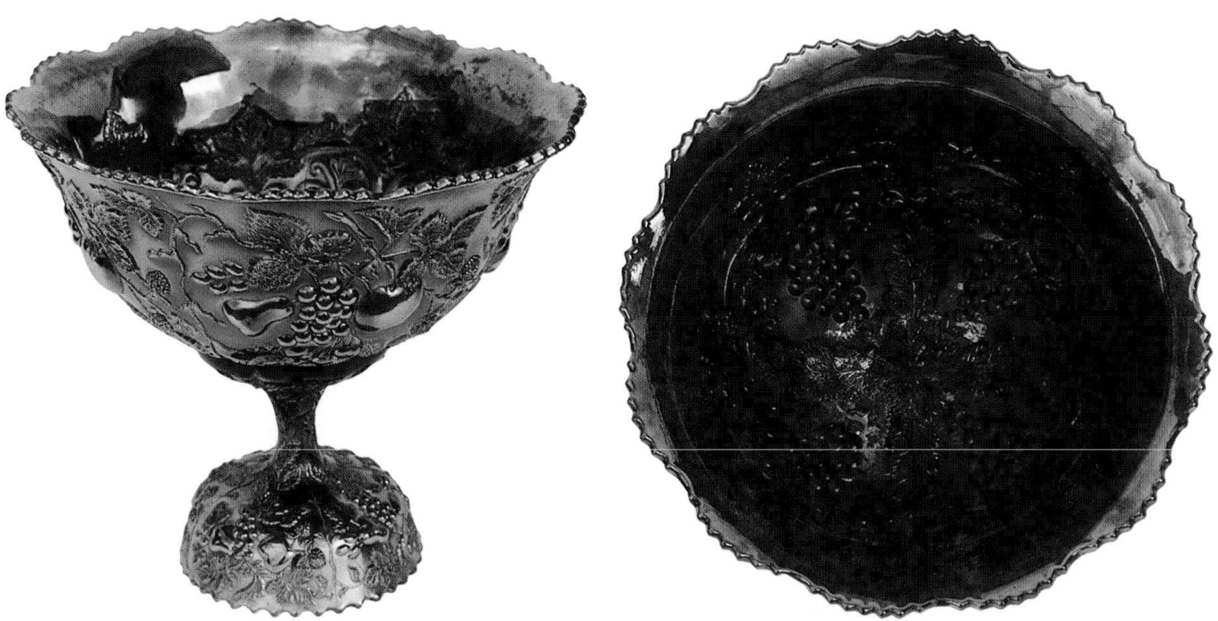

First found in 1987 by collectors, this rare variation of the Multi-Fruits and Flowers punch bowl has an inside pattern that has been named Scroll and Grape. Only the single example is reported. It is a beautiful pattern with acanthus leaves, clusters of grapes and leaves, and a border scroll. The piece is amethyst and both rare and desirable.

Seaweed Bowl (blue)

This is one of Millersburg's beautifully designed patterns found on bowls and plates. The example shown is a 10" bowl in ice cream shape in an extremely rare blue (the only one reported). In addition to this blue bowl, one in aqua is also known and it is equally as rare. The photo came from Ed Garner in the 1970s and is shown here for the first time.

Seaweed Chop Plate

Rare colors in Millersburg's Seaweed pattern include all blue items, small amethyst and marigold bowls, and marigold, amethyst, or green (shown) 10" plates. In addition the large ruffled bowl is found in clambroth and aqua and these excite Millersburg collectors. The 10" green plate shown has outstanding detail and iridescence with strong radium finish.

Seaweed Large Bowl (ICS)

In the Millersburg Seaweed large 10" ice cream shape bowl shown, both green and amethyst are rare, but even the marigold is difficult to find. In addition, a single blue example is reported and a single aqua is known. The Seaweed pattern lends itself nicely to bowls of this shape or to plates. It has a gracefulness that grabs us.

Singing Birds Mug Whimsey

Like so many whimsies, this is a one-of-a-kind item with great appeal. It was fashioned while the glass was still hot. The lip was formed into a spout, and turning a mug into a creamer. Perhaps it was simply a carry-home item some worker made for himself but in our time it is a real treasure.

Singing Birds Pitcher

Singing Birds is one of Northwood's better patterns. It is found in berry sets, table sets, water sets, a footed sherbet, and a mug. The green pitcher is one of the hardest items to find in this pattern. Some pieces in odd colors are equally scarce. There is a mug whimsied into a creamer that is also a rarity. Tumblers have been reproduced in several treatments so beware.

Spector's Department Store Plate

This is one of two well known advertising plates from the Fenton Art Glass Company that uses their Heart and Vine mould. The other is the Cooleemee, N.C. plate. The Cooleemee, N.C. plate is rarer, but the Spector's plate is equally sought. It says "Spector's Department Store" and measures about 9" across. Marigold is the only color.

Spirals and Spines

Only this single example of this trademarked Northwood vase has been reported and it is indeed rare and desirable. It is white carnival and has a spiral rib design similar to Ribbed Tornado. The California owner bought this vase at auction in 1996 and was given the privilege of naming it.

S-Repeat

Originally called National, this pattern was first introduced when Dugan was a part of the National Combine. Carnival shapes are more limited than other earlier types of glass and consist of a punch set, a whimsey creamer that was pulled from a punch cup, a covered sugar, and some questionable tumblers in marigold. Toothpick holders have been reproduced in carnival from the old moulds.

Stag and Holly

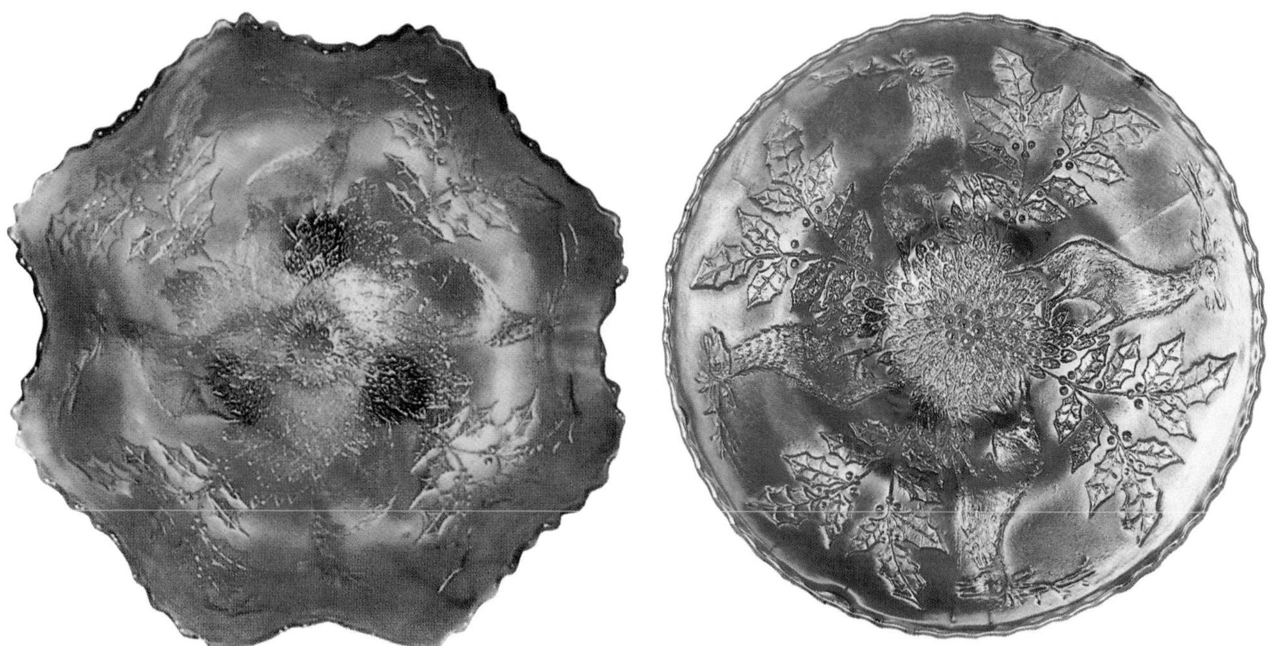

Shown are two pieces of Fenton's well-known Stag and Holly pattern, first made in 1912. Found in two sizes, the smaller has spatula feet while the larger has ball feet. Rare pieces include small and large plates, the giant rose bowl in blue or green, the large bowl in iridized milk glass, and the small bowl in red (shown along with a fantastic small marigold plate).

Stag and Holly Large Bowl

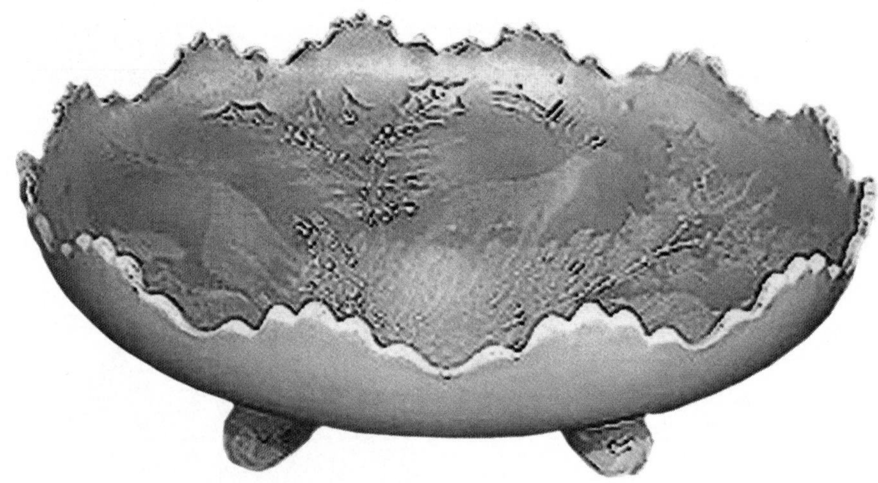

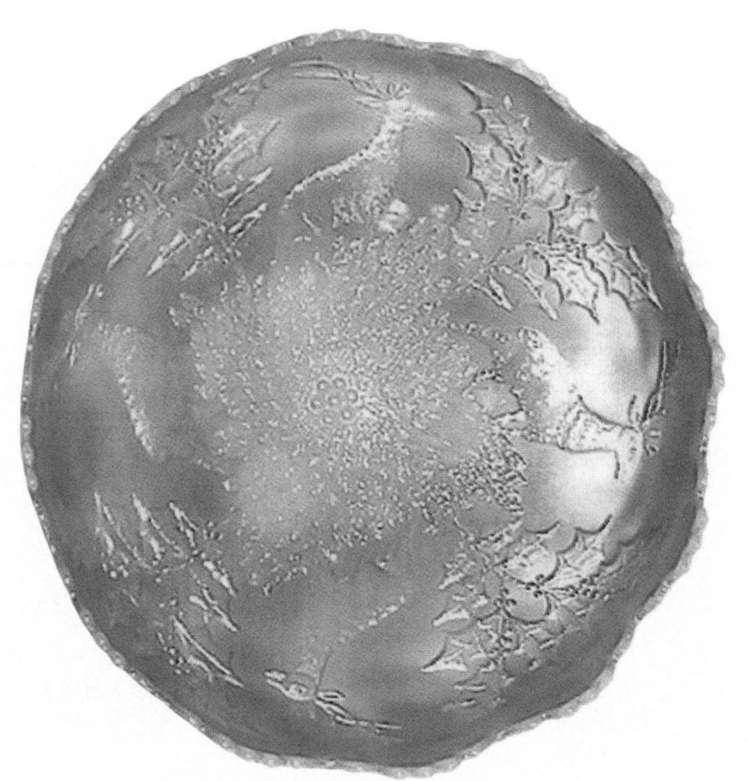

What a beauty this one-of-a-kind bowl is! It's the large bowl with ball feet that has been flared then pulled into an ice cream shape. The topper is marigold iridescence on moonstone glass. Isn't it amazing how imaginative the glassmakers were to try new treatments to punch up their lines? And aren't we all thrilled they did!

Starflower

This beautiful pitcher was produced by the Fenton Art Glass Company around 1911. It can usually be found in cobalt blue carnival, but on rare occasions a marigold and this very rare white example have shown up. No tumblers are known. All colors are considered hard to find. The design is molded flowers and leaves that climb up each panel. It is similar to other Fenton designs.

Stippled Diamonds

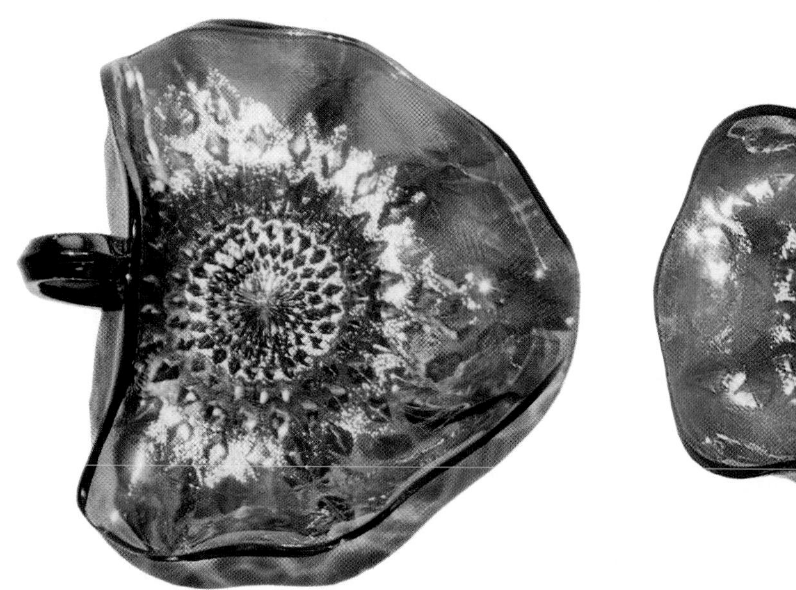

Here are two varieties of the same pattern from the Millersburg Glass Company. All examples of Stippled Diamonds have surfaced in the last four or five years. There are one vaseline and two green nappies and possibly two amethyst flattened bonbons called card trays. We strongly suspect a marigold piece will eventually show up, but until then, Millersburg collectors will have to be satisfied these five rare and desirable pieces.

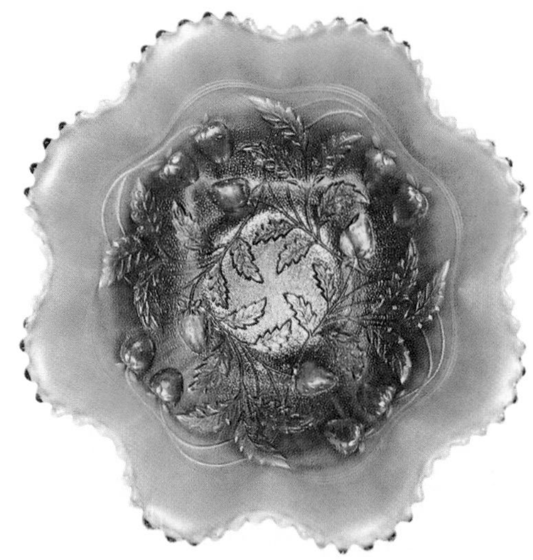

Strawberry

This Northwood pattern is quite familiar to most collectors. It is found in bowls and plates in a wide range of colors. It can have a plain background or a stippled background as shown. The color is a rare aqua opalescent that tends slightly to the green. It is an outstanding rarity, and the only example reported at this time.

Strawberry Plate (Stippled)

None of the colors found on this Northwood pattern on stippled plates are easy to find. The marigold, green, and cobalt blue shown are all rare and only the ice blue is rarer. Please note the plate has a band of three rings like all the stippled pieces, but the rest of the design is the same as non-stippled items.

Strawberry Scroll

Strawberry Scroll is another of Fenton's better water set patterns. It is found in marigold and blue. The pitcher is unique in shape with a pinched waist and a band of scrolling that divides the two strawberry patterns. Both pitchers and tumblers are difficult to find and desirable.

Strawberry Wreath Boat (vaseline)

Only the one example of this Millersburg whimsey has ever surfaced. It was whimsied from a small berry bowl with two sides pulled up high and the ends of the opposite sides turned down like a spout. It is called a gravy boat. The color is vaseline with marigold iridescence. It is very desirable.

Sunflower

This Northwood pattern is found on spatula footed bowls that measure about 8½". The Meander pattern covers the exterior. Colors are mostly marigold, amethyst, and green, but cobalt blue, teal, and Renninger blue (shown) show up rarely and bring high prices. And there is also a rumor of a marigold plate but it hasn't been confirmed.

Sunken Hollyhock Lamp

This is probably the most available of the carnival GWTW lamps. It can be found in a honey-marigold or the rich red carnival shown. It stands some 25" tall and has solid brass fittings. Often parts are found but to find a complete lamp with both shades is a hard task.

Superb Drape Vase

Several questions surround this beautiful vase, but certainly not its importance or rarity. It stands about 6½" tall and the simple design of waves of drapery are beautifully done. While many collectors credit this piece to the Northwood Company, we have no proof. It is known in one green example (shown), one marigold example, and two aqua opalescent ones.

Sweetheart

This was called Marjorie by Cambridge who listed it as their #2631 in crystal where it was found in several shapes. In carnival glass, it is known as Sweetheart. It can be found in rare marigold tumblers and marigold, green, and amethyst covered cracker jars.

Swirl Hobnail

Swirl Hobnail is one of Millersburg's prized patterns in rose bowls, a vase, and the spittoon shown. The majority of items found are marigold or amethyst, but here we show a very rare green spittoon. It is one of only three reported in this color (at least one of the others is badly damaged) and therefore is a prized treasure. Even the damaged one caused a bit of a stir at auction a few years ago.

Thin Rib Vase

The Thin Rib vase is from Northwood and can be found in three base sizes. The example shown here is the mid-size funeral vase with a 4½" diameter base. What makes it exceptional is the aqua opalescent color. We understand it is one of only three examples known in this size and color. The iridescence is spectacular, shading from the aqua base to a rich marigold and finally the milky opalescent top.

Thistle

Thistle is found on bowls, rare plates, the Horlacher bowls, and an experimental bowl that has etched thistles. Colors include marigold, amethyst, blue, green, amber, aqua, and vaseline for bowls, and marigold, amethyst, and green on the rare plates. Here is an amethyst plate with fine satin finish; it shows this Fenton design to its very best.

Threaded Butterflies

This very rare plate is a real mystery in many ways and deserves much more attention than it has received. The exterior of this spatula footed piece has the U.S. Glass Colorado pattern so we can speculate on its maker, but the interior pattern is a different matter. It is the first and only piece of this "butterflies" pattern found in carnival glass or any other type of glass. The color is a rich aqua with strong satin iridescence. The combination of butterflies, threading, feather scrolls, and scale-like flower petals is very unusual.

Three Fruits Medallion

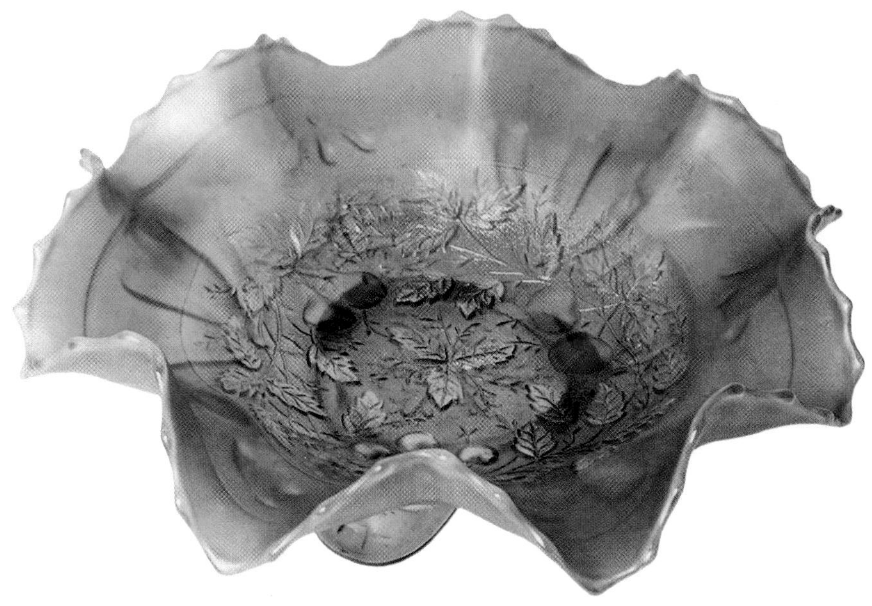

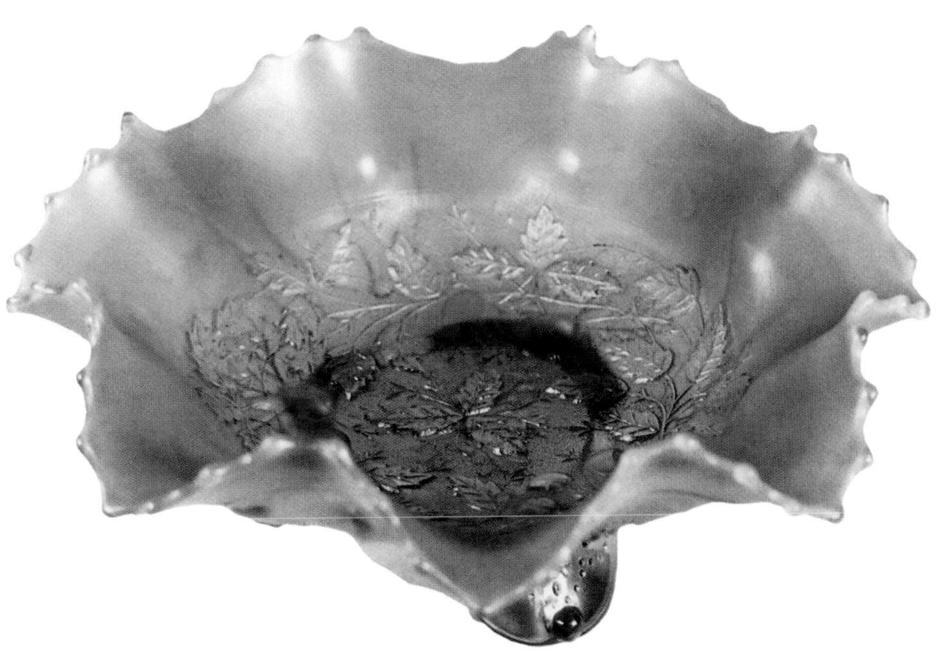

This Northwood pattern differs from the regular Three Fruits pattern in that it has a center medallion of three leaves. It is a pleasure to show the very rare lime green opalescent stippled bowl with spatula feet and the contrasting aqua opalescent bowl that isn't all that rare.

Three Fruits Stippled Plate

Plates in this well known Northwood pattern are very desirable and are found either with stippling in the center or without. Colors cover a wide range and include all the vivid colors as well as honey amber, lavender, horehound, teal, sapphire blue, ice blue, ice green, aqua opalescence, ice green opalescent, ice blue opalescent, and violet. Shown is a rare sapphire blue stippled plate.

Three Row Vase

Three Row is one of the better vase designs from the Imperial Glass Company. There is a variation that has two rows and is called the Two Row vase. Colors are purple, marigold, and the smoke shown (one of two or three known examples in this color). These vases stand 7½" – 8" tall and have a diameter of about 4". For years there have been rumors of a green Three Row vase but to date none have been verified.

Tomahawk

Shown in old Cambridge ads, this miniature novelty item is quite rare (it has been reproduced in other colors). It measures 7¼" long, is 2" wide, and is a rich cobalt blue.

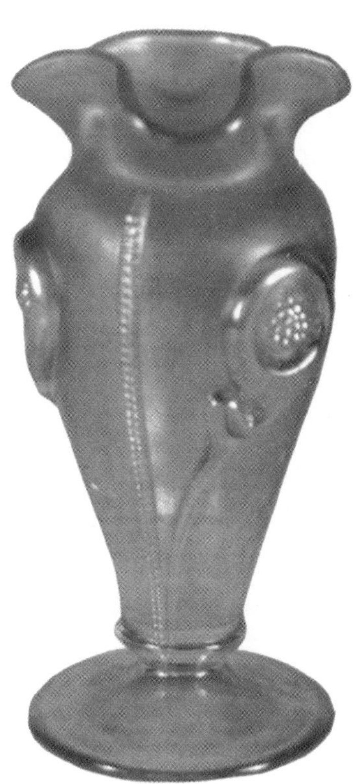

Tornado Variant

Just why there is this variation of the Northwood Tornado vase is a real mystery but here it is. Only two or three marigold vases have been reported. And while some collectors feel this vase is foreign, it would be hard to declare it so without more information.

Tornado Vase Whimsey

This rare version of the Tornado vase is called a "cone shaped whimsey" by collectors. It looks just like a pulled out regular vase except the base is a bit different. Colors are marigold, lavender (shown), and celeste blue with the last two showing some stretch effect to the glass.

Town Pump

One of Northwood's most popular novelties, this version came about in 1912. It is 6½" tall, sits on a sturdy collar base, and can be found in amethyst, marigold, and green. Few examples show up without some damage, especially spout or handle damage. This doesn't discourage collectors who would love to own one of these. All are rare with amethyst easiest to find.

Tracery

Tracery is unlike anything else the Millersburg Company produced. The exterior is plain and the bonbon can be oval or squared. The interior pattern is delicate daisy-like flowers connected by beading. Colors are either amethyst or green. Both are very desirable, but seldom sold.

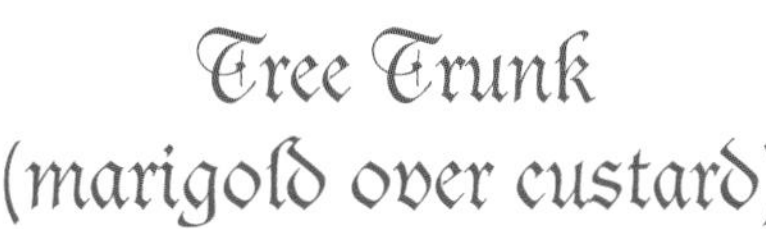

Tree Trunk (marigold over custard)

Here is another variation of treatment in this popular Northwood vase pattern. The example shown is a mid-size vase with a 4½" base diameter. It is a marigold iridization over custard glass. It is one of only three or four vases in this treatment.

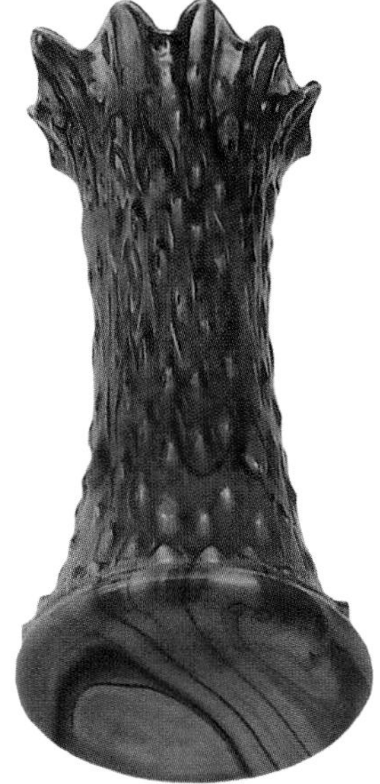

Tree Trunk Blue Slag Vase

Of all the rare colors and sizes in this Northwood vase pattern, this mid-size vase in iridized blue sage has to be one of the best. It is currently one of few items known in this process, and is simply spectacular in every way.

Tree Trunk Elephant's Foot Vase

Because of the large 5½" diameter base, this Tree Trunk vase is called an elephant's foot vase. It is extremely desirable and rare in all colors. One marigold, two or three green, and a handful of amethyst examples are known. These range in height from 7" to 10½". The top is often flared and ruffled giving them a greater width than height.

Tree Trunk Funeral Vase (ice green)

While ice green is found in all sizes of this vase, this 17½" tall funeral vase has to be one of the rarest. It has a base diameter of more than 5". It is a stunning example of Northwood's genius putting great patterns with rare colors. Please note this vase has a plunger base.

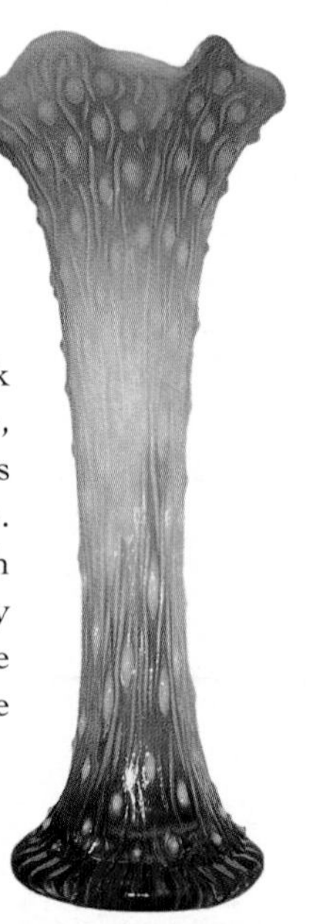

Tree Trunk Green Opalescent Vase

Unreported until we showed it on the back cover of our *Carnival Glass Encyclopedia, Eighth Edition,* this rare, one-of-a-kind vase is Northwood's Tree Trunk in the standard size. It is on green opalescent glass that has rich iridescence applied. The opalescence is very good and covers more than half the vase. The green seems slightly darker than those opalescent versions that are not iridized.

Tree Trunk Jardiniere

Not stretched or swung like the regular Elephant's Foot vase in the Tree Trunk pattern, this very rare vase is ruffled and flared into the jardiniere shape. It is a rich amethyst color. This vase whimsey has a massive look.

Tree Trunk JIP Vase

The Northwood Tree Trunk vase must have been a popular item because it was made in several sizes and shapings. The JIP shape (jack-in-the-pulpit) is one of the rarest with only one marigold and two amethyst examples reported so far. These are about 7" tall and were made from the standard vase mould with a base diameter of about 3½". The front is turned down while the back is turned up giving it its name. It is also called a Jester's Cup by some collectors.

Trefoil Finecut Plate (Millersburg)

The Trefoil Finecut pattern is normally found on the exterior of Millersburg Many Stars bowls, but here is the only reported iridized version *without* the interior pattern. It was shaped into a large plate. Both the interior and the exterior are iridized and the color is a rich marigold. Trefoil Finecut is also found in rare crystal bowls and plates without any iridescence. This single carnival example is the "best of the best" in this pattern. Please note there are three distinct patterns in the overall exterior design. The rim design and the marie (base) design are similar, while the central pattern is similar to honeycombing.

Trout and Fly Plate

Millersburg made such naturalistic fish and bird patterns (Big Fish, Nesting Swan, Trout and Fly) that the artists must have been real students of nature. The Trout and Fly bowls are favorites of collectors but the rare plates are in a class by themselves. Only two amethyst (one damaged) and one or two green ones reported.

Tulip Compote

Millersburg's Tulip mould was also used in the Flowering Vine compotes. This one has no interior design. These stand about 8½" tall, have a thin columned stem, and an octagonal base. One marigold, three amethyst, and two green are known. It is a very rich and stately piece. It is both rare and desirable but a bit less coveted than the Flowering Vine.

Venetian Giant Rose Bowl (lamp base)

This was originally called Kenneth when it was made by the Ohio Flint Glass Company in 1907. The mould moved to Jefferson Glass in 1908 when Ohio Flint closed and then to Millersburg in 1909. Millersburg is where this rare iridized version came about. It is also known in green as well as the marigold shown. When Millersburg closed, this mould was moved to Cambridge Glass where it was used for a crystal lamp base after 1914.

Venetian Table Set

This was originally called Kenneth when it was made by the Ohio Flint Glass Company in 1907. When the factory closed, John Fenton must have acquired some of the moulds for besides the well known giant rose bowl, this table set is found iridized in very limited amounts. The covered butter, cream, and covered sugar are the only pieces known. They are either marigold or clambroth with a radium finish.

Victorian (peach opalescent)

The Dugan Glass Company usually produced these large 10" – 12" ruffled bowls in amethyst, but here is a very rare peach opalescent example. Two have been reported and one of those is damaged. The design is quite good with a wedding ring look that has leaves and beaded buttons added.

Victorian Ice Cream Bowl

Most Victorian bowls are found ruffled but here is the exception — the only known ice cream shaped bowl in this pattern. It measures about 11" across. The iridescence is quite good with a satiny finish and vivid color. The shape is quite shallow with a rolled-up on the edges.

Vintage (Persian blue)

Vintage was one of Fenton's most prolific patterns. It is found in three sizes of bowls, three sizes of plates, two sizes of epergne, a fernery, wine glass, bonbon, and several whimsies. Red, aqua opalescent, celeste blue, vaseline, and Persian blue are favorite colors of collectors. The piece shown is a beautiful 10" ruffled bowl with heavy satin iridescence.

Vintage Banded Mug

First made in the early 1920s by the Diamond Glass Company, this pattern creates little excitement except for this rare, one-of-a-kind *amethyst* mug. Most pieces of this pattern are found in marigold although the mugs are also found in smoke and light green.

Vintage Bowl

Vintage was probably Fenton's answer to Northwood's Grape and Cable. It is found in large and small bowls, a bonbon or card tray with handles, a compote, a one-lily epergne, a three-footed fernery, a punch set, and four sizes of plates. The rarest items are the 9" aqua opalescent plate and the 9" aqua opalescent three-in-one bowl shown.

Vintage Fernery Whimsey Plate

This 10" footed whimsey plate is actually one piece most collectors could afford because it isn't valued as much as most items in this book. The rub is, it is the only example reported at this time. It was shaped from the ordinary Vintage fernery in cobalt blue. It is very beautiful with great iridescence.

Vintage/Hobnail Sauce

This 5½" sauce is rarer than the larger bowls in this Millersburg pattern. Seven or eight marigold, two blue, two amethyst, and two green have been reported. Bowls can be ruffled or ice cream shape, like the bowl shown. Generally speaking, small bowls are much harder to find in Millersburg patterns than larger bowls.

Vintage Sauce (Fenton)

This 5½" ruffled bowl in the Fenton Vintage pattern is a beauty. It is celeste blue, which along with red and aqua opalescent, is a top rarity in this pattern. If you look carefully you will see the edges have a good amount of stretching or onion skin and the iridescence is almost radium with a good deal of pink in the luster.

Waterlily and Cattails Pitcher (Northwood)

When you hear that color makes all the difference, it certainly applies to this pitcher. In marigold, it is a bit ordinary but in the only known cobalt blue pitcher, it is spectacular. It is very rare and very desirable. There are a few blue tumblers as well, and they are quite rare too.

Wheat (Northwood)

Found in only three shapes (all shown), this very rare pattern from Northwood is a bit of a mystery. To date only one covered bowl, one stemmed sherbet, and two sweetmeats are reported. All are found in amethyst and the second sweetmeat is green. Perhaps the design was considered unnecessary since it was made at the same time as Northwood's Grape and Cable, and therefore was dropped, but we just can't be sure. At any rate, all are rare and very desirable.

Wide Panel Epergne

First made by Northwood about 1909, this beautiful four-lily epergne is a massive and impressive item. Because of the way the lilies fit into their glass sleeves, many seen today have damage. Colors are green (easiest to find), marigold, amethyst, white, cobalt blue, ice green, ice blue, and an extremely rare aqua opalescent.

Wide Rib Vase (Northwood)

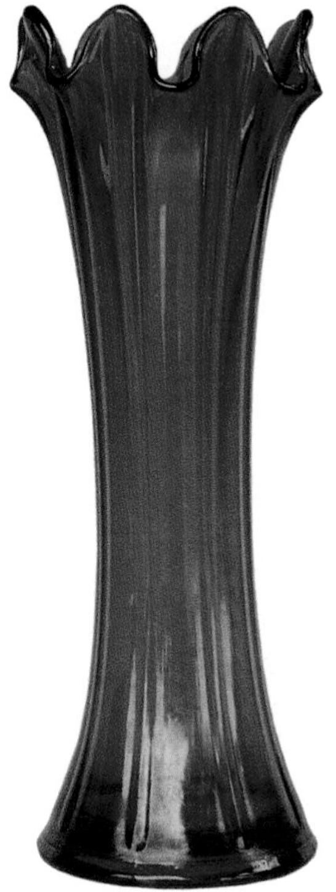

Although sometimes called Thin Rib by collectors, the Wide Rib name is more appropriate since there is another Northwood Thin Rib pattern. These vases are found in three base diameters and range in height from 5" to over 20". Shapes are usually flared but JIP shapes are known. Colors range from marigold, amethyst, blue, white, ice green, ice blue, teal, and russet to the unusual rare sapphire (shown), vaseline, and very rare aqua opalescent.

Wildflower Compote

This 6" jelly compote from the Millersburg Company, is a very desirable item. It can be found in marigold, amethyst, green, and vaseline. Known in either a deep straight compote or an open and flared one. The design is interesting with blossoms, leaves, and vine that wrap around the inside of the piece. The foot is always a clover-leaf base with a flute exterior. The original mould (minus the interior pattern) came from the Crystal Glass Company after it closed in 1908.

Wild Rose Lamps

When the Riverside Glass Company closed in 1907, John Fenton purchased a line of lamps called the Lucille line. This grouping contained four sizes of what we now call the Wild Rose lamp, a lamp Riverside called their Riverside Ladies, that is now known as Ladies Medallion lamp, and four sizes of the Colonial lamps that we now call Flute (these are found only in crystal). Except for the small handled lamp, the Wild Rose lamps were made in carnival glass in marigold, amethyst, and green, while the Ladies Medallion lamp is known in green and amethyst. Strangely, fragments of these lamps have been found at the Millersburg plant site in vaseline (shown).

Windflower (vaseline)

Generally speaking, this Diamond Glass Compnay pattern is easily found and not very costly, but there are exceptions. They are six, eight, and ten ruffled or ice cream shape bowls, plates, and a scarce one-handled nappy. Here is the rarest bowl of all and the only reported example in this color. It is vaseline and the color almost jumps off the glass.

Wishbone and Spades Chop Plate

Besides the smaller 7" plates found in the Dugan Wishbone and Spades pattern, there is also the magnificent 11" chop plate shown here. This large plate is also found in peach opalescent and these are even rarer than the purple examples. Wishbone and Spades was a short-lived pattern and the rarity of these plates attest to this fact.

Wisteria

Wisteria is probably the rarest of the Northwood water set patterns. Pitchers are white or ice blue, while the tumblers are found in white, ice blue, lime green, and ice green. In addition there is a green whimsey vase, made from a pitcher and a white whimsey bank fashioned from the tumbler mould. The design of flowers vining over a lattice is very realistic.

Woodpecker and Ivy

Like the Acorn vase and the Blackberry Bark vase, this beautiful rarity is now considered to be from the Millersburg Glass Company. Shards of the Woodpecker and Ivy vase have been found at the Millersburg plant site and that is pretty strong evidence. At any rate, examples in marigold, green, and vaseline have been documented with the green one reportedly broken. Here we show the beautiful marigold one and as anyone can see, the shape is much like the Acorn vase. On one side is a solid glass woodpecker and the rest of the vase shows a bark-like pattern with vines and flowers trailing just below the scalloped top.

Wreath of Roses Spittoon Whimsey (Dugan)

This pattern was apparently made over a long period of time — first by Dugan and then by Diamond. Wreath of Roses can easily be found in a rose bowl or a tri-cornered whimsey bowl all from the same mould. The spittoon whimsey is another thing however for only two are reported — one in marigold and the beautiful lavender example shown. To take the ordinary rose bowl shape and whimsey it into this very beautiful spittoon shape shows how skilled glassmarkers were (and are). And to then produce so few of such beauties that they are rare today, boggles the mind.

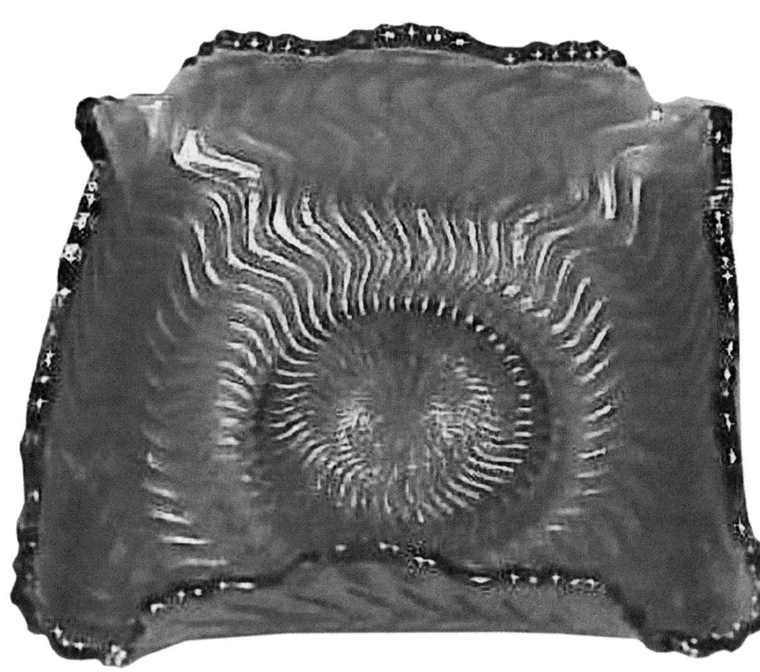

Zig Zag Square Sauce

This Millersburg piece is actually a double rarity for it is the first sauce reported and it is square. It has a very rich marigold finish and the luster is a typical Millersburg radium.

Zippered Heart

Zippered Heart, Imperial's #292, was made in crystal in 1909 and in carnival glass in 1911. It is one of their most impressive patterns. It can be found on berry sets, marigold and purple 5" vases, emerald green 9" vases (often called rose bowls), and purple and green 9" ruffled top vases, called Queen's Vases. All the vase shapes are extremely rare and very desirable to collectors. We're happy to show the marigold 5" vase and the emerald 9" vase.